JOURNEY
THROUGH THE
BIBLE

A Book-by-Book Overview

Journey Through the Bible
A Book-by-Book Overview

JOURNEY
THROUGH THE
BIBLE

A Book-by-Book Overview

by

J. Ralph Brewer

FIRST PRINTING 1979
SECOND PRINTING 1983

Library of Congress Catalog Card Number: 79-90350
International Standard Book Number: 0-87148-450-1

Copyright © 1979
Pathway Press
Cleveland, Tennessee 37311

Printed in the United States of America

DEDICATION

This book is affectionately dedicated to my uncle, the Reverend J. R. Brewer, for whom I am named and to whom I am indebted for his shining Christian example. A minister of the gospel for more than forty years, he has borne well the torch of faith, clearly marking the path for all to see. His study of the Bible, his commitment to God, and his love for people have made him a preacher-pastor *par excellence* and have endeared him to a multitude.

INTRODUCTION

In underscoring the value of the Bible, John Quincy Adams, fourth president of the United States, is reported to have said, "The Bible is the Book of all others, to be read at all ages, and in all conditions of life. . . . It is an invaluable and inexhaustible mine of knowledge and virtue."

This text is based upon the premise that the Bible is indeed the "Book of all others" and that it is in fact the very foundation for all Christian faith. Through its sacred contents we come to understand God, to understand the revelation of His will for mankind, and to enter into a meaningful and joyful relationship with Him through faith in His Son, Jesus Christ.

It is one thing, however, to applaud the merits of the Scriptures and quite another to dig consistently into its pages, to discover its life-giving principles, and to apply them to everyday experience. Through the emphasis of this volume, it is the author's hope that Bible reading and Bible study will be identified as a normal pattern of Christian living and that the reader will be challenged to a greater personal commitment in researching the Word of God.

This text is not designed as an exhaustive analysis of the books of the Bible, but is merely an attempt to capture the highlights of each one and to present them in capsule form. With this in mind, you will observe that the action is swift; every page is jammed with bits of information which can be referred to again and again.

Remember as you journey through the Bible to pause long enough at each juncture to allow the Holy Spirit to fully illuminate your mind and heart and to open the rich treasures of God's Book to you in a personal way.

Author

CONTENTS

UNIT 1

GENESIS

Author	Date of Writing	Theme	Key Personalities	Main Events
Moses	1450-1410 B.C.	Beginnings	Adam, Eve, Noah, Abraham, Isaac, Jacob, Joseph	Creation, Fall of Man, Great Flood, Tower of Babel, Origin and Early History of Israel

Genesis is one of the most fascinating and intriguing of the Old Testament books. It is sometimes referred to as the Introduction or Preface to the Bible. In this light, it seems most fitting that the inspired record begins with those simple but powerful words, "In the beginning God."

Genesis is the first book of the Law (or Pentateuch), and its authorship is usually ascribed to Moses: It is believed to have been written during the period of wilderness wanderings of the young Hebrew nation. The English word *genesis* comes by way of Latin, from the Greek, and means "origin" or "beginning." Thus, the name of the book provides an excellent clue to its contents. Genesis is a book of beginnings—the beginning of everything but God, who is eternal. Genesis records the beginning of the world: plant, animal, and human life, civilization, nations and languages, marriage and family, sin and crime, sorrow and death, sacrifice and salvation.

The Book of Genesis opens with what is known as the "hymn of creation" or the "poem of the dawn" and closes with Joseph's funeral service in the land of Egypt. Sandwiched between these two important events are several millennia of exciting history. As you peruse the pages of this book, you will meet the world's first man—Adam, the world's oldest man—Methuselah, and the first man to ever go to heaven without dying—Enoch. You will share the adventures of Noah as he and his family survive a devastating flood. You will listen with rapt attention as God calls Abraham to be the father of His chosen people. You will watch with tense emotion as a teenage dreamer rises above the ostracism and persecution of his own brothers to sit on the throne of Egypt.

But keep in mind as you meet these interesting personalities and share their successes and failures that Genesis is more than a document of history. It is the record of God's relationship to the human race. Interwoven into the fabric of this first book of the Bible are the threads of many major doctrines of the Scriptures—the Doctrine of the Creator—God (Genesis 1:1), the Doctrine of the Trinity (Genesis 1:26), the Doctrine of Redemption Through a Promised Messiah (Genesis 3:15), the Judgment of God (Genesis 6:3), the Doctrine of Grace (Genesis 6:8), and the Doctrine of Justification by Faith (Genesis 15:6). Little wonder Genesis is called the "seed plot of the Bible."

EXODUS

Author	Date of Writing	Theme	Key Personalities	Main Events
Moses	1450-1410 B.C.	Deliverance of Israel From Egyptian Slavery	Moses	Life Story of Moses, Ten Plagues, Exodus of Israel From Egypt, Wilderness Experiences, Giving of the Law, Institution of Tabernacle Worship

Exodus is the second book of the Law (or Pentateuch). Its author is Moses and, like Genesis, it was probably written during the forty years of wandering in the Wilderness. Designed as a sequel to Genesis, the Book of Exodus continues the history of the Jewish people. While Genesis traces their ancestral roots, Exodus records the actual beginning of the Hebrew nation.

Exodus derives its name from the Septuagint (Greek version) of the Old Testament. The word *exodus* means "the going out"; thus, the name of the book is descriptive of its contents.

Exodus may be subdivided into three principle parts using three key words: slavery (Exodus 1:1-12:36), emancipation (Exodus 12:37-18:27), and revelation (Exodus 19:1-40:38). The first part of Exodus vividly describes the relentless and cruel oppression of the Hebrews by the Egyptians, their agonizing cries for deliverance, and God's answer through the great man Moses. The second part of the book records the emancipation of this mass of slaves from Egyptian servitude and the beginning of a forty-year journey in the Wilderness before attempting the conquest of Canaan. The third section of the book describes the revelation of God's plan and purpose for the nation of Israel through the giving of the Law on Mt. Sinai and the establishment of a significant system of worship.

In Genesis we were introduced to many outstanding personalities—Adam, Enoch, Noah, Abraham, Isaac, Jacob, and Joseph. But in Exodus there is only one towering personality—Moses. He is one of the most celebrated men in Israel's history and one of the greatest men to live before Christ. He is noted as a leader *par excellence,* possessing deep compassion for his people. Stephen paid tribute to him in the New Testament by saying, "[He] was learned in all the wisdom of the Egyptians, and was mighty in words and in deeds" (Acts 7:22).

In addition to the historical aspects of the book, Exodus also contains several important doctrinal themes. The theme of Redemption is beautifully illustrated in the Passover ceremony and in Israel's deliverance from the bondage of Egypt. The killing of the sacrificial lamb and the sprinkling of its blood foretell of the New Testament "Lamb of God, which taketh away the sin of the world" (John 1:29). The giving of the Law on Mt. Sinai serves to remind us that Christ is the true Lawgiver and Mediator of the everlasting covenant. The establishment of worship as a part of the private and national life of the Hebrew people (symbolized in the erection of the tabernacle) emphasizes that God forever seeks to have fellowship and communion with those whom He loves.

LEVITICUS

Author	Date of Writing	Theme	Key Personalities	Main Events
Moses	1450-1410 B.C.	Holiness	Moses, Aaron (the High Priest)	Instituting the Sacrificial System, Consecration of the Priests, Sacrilege of Nadab and Abihu, Jewish Religious Festivals

Leviticus is the third book of the Pentateuch and is so called because it relates principally to the Levites and priests and their services. It served as a kind of "Minister's Handbook" for the priesthood and aided them in carrying out prescribed regulations for personal cleanliness, diagnosing and classifying diseases, and implementing worship procedures.

Moses is credited as the author. Fifty-six times in Leviticus it is recorded that the Lord spoke directly to Moses, giving him the message to write. Jesus also acknowledged Moses as the author of Leviticus in Mark 1:44.

Leviticus continues the history, organization, and development of the chosen nation, with special emphasis upon the religious aspect. Leviticus is concerned chiefly with the arrangement of the sanctuary and the life which God requires of those who bear His name and who fellowship with Him. The theme of Leviticus is *holiness,* a term occurring more often in this book than in any other book of the Bible. Sacrifice is an inescapable demand as you read this book. The word *sacrifice* occurs 42 times; *priest* is found 189 times; *blood* 86 times; *holy* 87 times; and *atonement* 45 times. The New Testament makes reference to the Book of Leviticus about 90 times.

Leviticus focuses upon three major ideas: (1) the holiness of God, (2) the sinfulness of man, and (3) the provisions for access to God for sinful man. The keynote of the book is found in Leviticus 19:2—"Ye shall be holy: for I the Lord your God am holy."

The Book of Leviticus outlines a very elaborate system of rituals, ceremonies, and sacrifices for approaching God. However, when viewed in the light of the New Testament, especially the Epistle to the Hebrews, we discover that these were but a shadow of good things to come and "a figure for the time then present" (Hebrews 9:9). Jesus Christ, our High Priest, "hath . . . obtained a more excellent ministry" and "he is the mediator of a better covenant, which was established upon better promises" (Hebrews 8:6).

NUMBERS

Author	Date of Writing	Theme	Key Personalities	Main Events
Moses	1450-1410 B.C.	The Consequences of Unbelief	Moses, Aaron, Miriam, Joshua, Caleb, Korah, Balaam	Numbering of Israel, Murmuring of the People, Sin of Miriam, Rebellion of Korah, Twelve Spies, Story of Balaam

The fourth book of the Law (or Pentateuch) is Numbers. Like the other three books, its authorship is also ascribed to Moses. Numbers receives its name from the two numberings of the children of Israel recorded in chapters 1 through 4 and in chapter 26. The first census was taken while camped at Sinai; the second occurred some thirty-nine years later on the plains of Moab, just prior to marching into Canaan. Aside from these two events, however, the book has little to do with numbers and deals primarily with the experiences of the young Hebrew nation during the forty years of wandering in the Wilderness.

After the miraculous victory over Pharaoh's army at the Red Sea, Moses faced many serious problems in trying to lead this horde of newly freed slaves to the "Land of Promise." Not among the least of these was the responsibility of providing for basic personal needs—food, water, and shelter—to say nothing of national concerns such as establishing law and order, securing and training an army for defense, and developing a workable system of government. Added to Moses' leadership burden was the daily task of listening to the critical outpourings of a bitter and discontented people.

The people complained about everything from the diet to the desert and longed to return to the land of Egypt. God viewed the critical spirit of the people not as an affront to the leadership of Moses, but as sin and rebellion against Him.

Consequently, judgment was sent upon them on several occasions.

Perhaps the greatest tragedy of the people was their failure to believe the promise of God and to possess the land of Canaan. Because of this faithlessness and their refusal to trust God, the entire generation was condemned to wandering in the Wilderness for nearly forty years. The entire adult generation (except Caleb and Joshua) died without seeing the fulfillment of a long-awaited dream.

While Numbers is a "Book of Murmurings," it is also a "Book of Miracles." Throughout the book, God's grace and providential care are actively demonstrated. The manna from heaven, the water from a barren rock, the guiding cloud, the brazen serpent for healing—all reflect the miraculous intervention of God for His people and His deep and abiding concern for them.

In Numbers 6:24-26 is found one of the most beautiful and best known passages, the Levitical Benediction:

> "The Lord bless thee, and keep thee:
> The Lord make his face shine upon thee,
>   and be gracious unto thee:
> The Lord lift up his countenance upon thee,
>   and give thee peace."

DEUTERONOMY

Author	Date of Writing	Theme	Key Personality	Main Events
Moses	1410 B.C.	Remember	Moses	Three Addresses of Moses, Song of Moses, Death of Moses

Deuteronomy is the fifth and final Book of the Law (or Pentateuch). The word *deuteronomy* means "second law" or "repetition of the law." While the Book of Deuteronomy contains a review of the Law received at Sinai, it is actually an amplified version.

Deuteronomy has always been highly regarded among the Jewish people as a book of deep spiritual value. Often quoted and referred to, it has served to guide the nation of Israel in crisis times. Deuteronomy was the lost book found in the days of King Josiah which brought spiritual reform to Israel (2 Kings 22, 23). New Testament writers quoted directly from the book thirty-two times and made eighty additional references to it. Its spiritual value is strongly emphasized by Jesus who quoted from it three times in routing the devil during His period of temptation (Luke 4:1-13).

The key word is *remember* which Moses used over and over again to remind the people how God delivered them from Egypt, led them through the Wilderness, and made of them a great nation. The book covers the short period between the end of Israel's wilderness wanderings and their entrance into Canaan. During this time, Moses delivered three great addresses to prepare the people mentally and spiritually to enter in and possess the land God promised to their forefathers.

The addresses of Moses may be summed up with three key phrases:

Retrospect—The past (first address)

Introspect—The present (second address)

Prospect—The future (third address)

In his first address, Moses reviewed the highlights of the forty-year wilderness experience. He reminded his people that in spite of the sin and unbelief of their fathers, God's faithful hand had guided them to the borders of the Promised Land. By reviewing both the success and failures of the past, Moses hoped to inspire vision and strong resolve for the future.

Moses' second and largest address (twenty-two chapters) was designed to acquaint a brand-new generation with the covenant God had made with Israel at Sinai. The older generation (with the exception of Joshua and Caleb) died in the Wilderness. If the sacred Law was to be perpetuated, it had to be reviewed, renewed, and obeyed. In this address, Moses not only restated the Ten Commandments but added what is known as the "Great Commandment"—"Thou shalt love the Lord thy God with all thine heart, and with all thy soul, and with all thy might" (Deuteronomy 6:5).

Moses' final address was prophetic in nature and looked to the future when Israel would possess the land of Canaan. The people were challenged to be faithful and obedient. As a result, God's manifold blessings were to be upon them. However, he also warned that if they were disobedient and unfaithful, terrible judgments would be visited upon them.

At the age of 120, Moses gave his last public charge to Israel and commended them to God's unfailing care. After appointing Joshua as his successor, the aged leader completed his writings and commanded that they be placed in the Ark of the Covenant to be read to the people every seven years. After composing a beautiful song of worship and praise, God called Moses to Mount Nebo where he died. With his passing, Israel lost a great leader, statesman, general, legislator, author, prophet, and intercessor.

REVIEW — UNIT 1

(Genesis—Deuteronomy)

1. What is the Pentateuch?

2. Who is the author?

3. Give the theme of each book.

4. Discuss the main events of each book.

5. Identify the following personalities:

Adam	Moses	Joshua
Enoch	Aaron	Jacob
Noah	Nadab and Abihu	Korah
Abraham	Miriam	Balaam
Isaac	Joseph	Balak

6. Name the ten plagues.

7. Give the Ten Commandments.

8. Quote the Levitical Benediction.

9. What is known as the "Great Commandment"?

10. What are the three key words used to describe the Book of Exodus?

Fill in the Blank:

1. The Book of Genesis opens with what is known as _____ or _____.

2. One scriptural doctrine introduced in Genesis is _____.

3. The word *genesis* means _____ or _____.

4. The word *exodus* means _____.

5. The Law was given to Moses on Mt. _____.

6. The theme of Redemption is illustrated in the _____ ceremony.

7. The word _____ occurs eighty-seven times in the Book of Leviticus.

8. The children of Israel wandered in the Wilderness for approximately _____ years.

9. The two men who survived the wilderness wandering and were permitted to go into the land of Canaan were _____ and _____.

10. The name *Deuteronomy* means _____ or _____.

11. The key word in Deuteronomy is _____.

12. Moses died at the age of _____.

UNIT 2

JOSHUA

Author	Date of Writing	Theme	Key Personalities	Main Events
Joshua	1400-1370 B.C.	The Conquest of Canaan	Joshua, Rahab, Achan	Crossing of the Jordan, Battle of Jericho, Story of Rahab, Achan's Sin, Gibeonite Treaty, Joshua Commanding Sun to Stand Still, Dividing the Land

After the death of Moses, Joshua (the son of Nun) became the leader of Israel. Moses had led his nation of slaves out of Egypt, through the forty years of Wilderness wandering to the borders of Canaan. However, because of his sin at Meribah, God permitted Moses to go no further. The task of entering, conquering, and settling the Promised Land was to be left in the hands of his capable and brave successor, Joshua.

Joshua was well qualified to assume the reins of leadership, having been Moses' assistant and confidant for some time. He served as his personal attendant during the period of Sinai (Exodus 24:13). As a military leader, he successfully commanded the Israelite forces against the Amalekites at Rephidim (Exodus 17:8-16). He was also one of the twelve spies who scouted out the land of Canaan and along with Caleb opposed the majority report not to try to conquer the land (Numbers 14:6-9). Joshua's outstanding qualities were faith, courage, obedience, and deep devotion to the law of God. His name means "Jehovah is salvation" and is indicative of his abundant trust in Jehovah God as Israel's ultimate hope and deliverance.

The Book of Joshua begins the second natural division of the Old Testament—the Historical Books. Twelve in number, the Historical Books cover the period of history from the establishment of the Hebrew homeland to the time the nation was destroyed (approximately 1,055 years).

The Book of Joshua itself covers a period of twenty-five to thirty years and may be subdivided into the following three parts:
1. Entering the land of Canaan (Joshua 1:1-5:15)
2. Conquering the land (Joshua 6:1-12:24)
3. Dividing the land (Joshua 13:1-24:33)

Thus, the book is basically the story of the conquest and settlement of Canaan. It is marked, however, by fierce and bloody conflict between the Israelites and the Canaanites. Thirty-one kings and their tribes were defeated in rapid succession in such miraculous ways as to remind the Israelites that their victories were not the result of military strength or strategy but of direct intervention by the Captain of the Lord of Hosts. The unquestioned triumph of the Israelites over the Canaanites illustrated the faithfulness of God in fulfilling the promise made to their forefathers hundreds of years before.

One interesting incident in the Book of Joshua is that of Rahab and her family. Prior to the Jericho invasion Rahab had risked her own life to protect two Hebrew spies sent to survey the city. In gratitude, the spies promised her safety if she would hang a scarlet cord from her window. This she did, and as a result, she and her family were the only survivors of the Jericho attack. Because of her faith in the God of Israel and the Hebrew cause, she is listed among the heroines of faith in the Epistle to the Hebrews (Hebrews 11:31). Following the fall of Jericho, she became the wife of Salmon, the mother of Boaz, and thereby became one of the ancestors of Jesus Christ (Matthew 1:5).

The book closes with the farewell addresses of Joshua in which he recalled the hand of God in Israel's history and challenged the people to serve God faithfully. He is perhaps best known for the statement, "Choose you this day whom ye will serve . . . but as for me and my house, we will serve the Lord" (Joshua 24:15). Joshua died in Shechem at the ripe old age of 110, having done a great work for God.

JUDGES

Author	Date of Writing	Theme	Key Personalities	Main Events
Unknown (Possibly Samuel)	1050-1000 B.C	Obedience to God brings life and peace. Disobedience brings oppression and death.	Gideon, Samson, Other Judges	Wars With Canaanite Enemies

The 300-year period covered by the Book of Judges is often referred to as the "Dark Ages" in Israel's history. This designation is the result of the unparalleled spiritual and moral declension that characterized the period.

Following the death of Joshua, a new generation arose which soon forgot God. Disregarding the laws he had established for their own good, they chose instead to follow the evil practices of their Canaanite neighbors. Intermarrying with them (which itself was a direct violation of God's law), the Hebrew nation quickly became corrupted by Canaanite influences and lapsed into frequent periods of apostasy and idolatry. The last verse of the book summarizes the attitude of the people and the times—"In those days there was no king in Israel: every man did that which was right in his own eyes" (Judges 21:25).

The Book of Judges records at least six periods of apostasy, with six occasions of oppression by their enemies and six deliverances. In studying the book, you will note the following three recurring phrases which identify these cycles:

1. "And the children of Israel did evil again in the sight of the Lord"
2. "And . . . [the Lord] sold them into the hands of their enemies round about"
3. "And when the children of Israel cried unto the Lord, the Lord raised up a deliverer . . . who delivered them."

Altogether there were thirteen judges (not including Eli and Samuel) who rose to the occasion to deliver Israel from her oppressors. None of them, however, ruled over the entire twelve tribes and none ever set up a dynasty or was succeeded by an heir to his judgeship. Since there was no centralized government at the time, some of the judges ruled simultaneously.

The judges of this period are not to be thought of as legal officials who settled disputes or decided points of law. They were primarily military chieftains who rallied the people of one particular tribe to overthrow their enemies. By virtue of their military exploits and their popularity among their own tribesmen, they were able to exert some degree of political control and influence. Gideon and Samson are perhaps the most colorful and best known of all the judges. The six periods of servitude and the corresponding judge(s) of each period are listed in the chart below:

JUDGES OF ISRAEL

Period	Oppressor	Length of Servitude	Judge	Length of Judgeship
1st Servitude	Mesopotamia	8 years	Othniel	40 years
2nd Servitude	Moab	18 years	Ehud	80 years
			Shamgar	
3rd Servitude	Jabin and Sisera	20 years	Deborah and Barak	40 years
4th Servitude	Midian	7 years	Gideon	40 years
			Abimelech	3 years
			Tola	23 years
			Jair	22 years
5th Servitude	Ammon	18 years	Jephthah	6 years
			Ibzan	7 years
			Elon	10 years
			Abdon	8 years
6th Servitude	Philistines	40 years	Samson	20 years

Eli and Samuel are also regarded as judges—Eli, the priest judge, and Samuel, the prophet judge (1 Samuel 1-10).

RUTH

Author	Date of Writing	Theme	Key Personalities	Main Events
Unknown (Possibly Samuel)	1000 B.C.	All things work to- gether for good to those who love God.	Ruth, Naomi, Boaz	Tragedies in Naomi's Family, Ruth's Love for Naomi, Ruth Meets and Marries Boaz.

Regarded as one of the choicest idyls of literature, the Book of Ruth is a classic romance that has charmed millions throughout the centuries. It is a refreshing and beautiful account of a young Moabite girl named Ruth who, after a series of family tragedies including the death of her husband, met and married a wealthy Hebrew farmer named Boaz. Through her marriage to Boaz, Ruth was given a new life and her past sorrow was turned to profound joy. The Book of Ruth is an inspiring story with a happy ending. It is a story of love in its purest form, of courage in the face of difficulty, and of faith's triumph over the harsh realities of life. More importantly, it is a grand demonstration of God's special concern for those who love Him, and a perfect example of the New Testament truth—"All things work together for good to them that love God" (Romans 8:28).

The setting for the book is the latter part of the twelfth century B.C. during the period of the judges. In sharp contrast to the idolatry and unfaithfulness of the times, the Book of Ruth focuses upon the faithfulness of one Jewish family. It reveals their quiet strength and humble dedication to God, despite the worst of circumstances. The book also provides some interesting glimpses into the customs and domestic life-style of the people during this period of Israel's history.

The best known and perhaps most loved passage in this brief book is Ruth's statement of devotion to her mother-in-law Naomi:

"Intreat me not to leave thee, or to return from follow-ing after thee: for whither thou goest, I will go; and where thou lodgest, I will lodge: thy people shall be my people, and thy God my God: Where thou diest, will I die, and there will I be buried: the Lord do so to me, and more also, if ought but death part thee and me" (Ruth 1:16, 17).

These sincere and deeply moving words are regarded by many as the most beautiful expression of love in all literature. Consequently, they have found a well-deserved place in Christian wedding ceremonies, ever increasing in beauty and charm each time they are repeated.

Ruth's beautiful pledge not only included loyalty to Naomi but to Naomi's God. She never again served the Moabite god, Chemosh, who was worshiped by human sacrifice. She, like Rahab, chose to cast her lot with the Hebrew people and to embrace their faith. Through this spiritual union, she was signally honored by God. Although a Gentile, she became the ancestress of kings, including the King of kings, Jesus Christ. Ruth is one of the four women mentioned in the genealogy of Christ in Matthew's Gospel. To her marriage with Boaz was added a son, Obed. Obed became the father of Jesse, who was the father of King David. Through this royal line, Jesus was born to be the Savior of all men, Jew and Gentile alike.

Great-grandmother to King David . . . ancestress of Jesus Christ. That is Ruth's story. What a bright conclusion to a story with a bleak beginning! Faith in God always triumphs.

1 SAMUEL

Author	Date of Writing	Theme	Key Personalities	Main Events
Samuel and Others (1 Samuel 10:25, 1 Chronicles 29:29)	930 B.C. and Later	The Effects of Sin in Relation to Israel and Her Leaders	Samuel, Saul, David, Jonathan	Eli's Judgeship, Life and Leadership of Samuel, Israel's First King—Saul, Beginning of David's Reign

The events of 1 Samuel cover a period of about 115 years and represent a continuation of the national history of the Hebrew nation. The Book of 1 Samuel begins where the Book of Judges ends. Eli and Samuel were the last in the succession of judges. Upon the conclusion of Samuel's judgeship, Israel entered upon a new form of government with the crowning of its first king.

The two Books of Samuel originally formed a single book. They were first divided in the Septuagint, an early Greek translation of the Scriptures. Samuel is generally regarded as the author of the major portion of 1 Samuel. However, since his death is recorded in chapter 25, he could not have written the remainder. There is some speculation that Nathan or Gad (1 Samuel 10:25, 1 Chronicles 29:29) may have completed the writing.

The Book of 1 Samuel divides itself into the biographies of three prominent men—Samuel (chapters 1-7), Saul (chapters 8-15), and David (chapters 16-31).

Samuel, whose birth was the result of the earnest prayers of his mother Hannah, is one of the towering spiritual figures of the Old Testament. His name means "asked of God." At an early age Hannah brought him to the tabernacle at Shiloh and dedicated him to the service of the Lord. There he grew under the tutorship of Eli the priest and participated in the various ministrations of worship. Samuel is generally regarded as the first of the great prophets, and his life is marked by deep devotion to God. As a man of exemplary prayer, he interceded for Israel on several occasions (1 Samuel 7:5-10, 8:6, 12:19-23) and was in the forefront in calling the nation to spiritual renewal.

The greatest disappointment of Samuel's life was the people's request—"Make us a king to judge us like all the nations" (8:5). This request constituted a rejection of the theocracy (rule of God) established by Moses and brought about the institution of the monarchy (rule of kings). With great reluctance Samuel bowed to the demand of the people and anointed Saul, the son of Kish, to be Israel's first king.

Few men have started their careers with more in their favor and have ended them in more bitter tragedy than did Saul. His story stands in the pages of the Old Testament as an unforgettable witness to the tragic results of disobedience and self-will. His consuming desire for popularity coupled with fits of rage and jealousy alienated most of his close friends and supporters and ultimately led to his downfall. The death of Saul and his three sons—Jonathan, Abinadab, and Melchishua—in the battle with the Philistines on Mt. Gilboa for all practical purposes ended the reign of the household of Saul and paved the way for the long and illustrious career of King David.

Among the more interesting highlights of 1 Samuel are the stories of David and Goliath, Saul and the witch of Endor, and the noble friendship of Jonathan and David.

2 SAMUEL

Author	Date of Writing	Theme	Key Personalities	Main Events
Samuel and Others	930 B.C. and Later	The Effects of Sin in Relation to Israel and Her Leaders	David, Ishbosheth, Abner, Joab, Bathsheba, Absalom	David's Coronation in Judah, Civil War in Israel, David Becomes King Over the Nation, Military Campaigns, David's Great Sin and Its Consequences

The Book of 2 Samuel is the record of the forty-year reign of King David. In 1 Samuel David appears as a rising star in Israel's future, but in 2 Samuel he attains the full stature of his leadership as the king of the nation. David accepted the crown at the young age of thirty and was to become the greatest of Israel's kings. His reign was characterized by many notable achievements and is often referred to as the "Golden Age" of Israel's history.

Upon the death of Saul, David became the king of Judah, establishing his capital in Hebron. He did not immediately receive the allegiance of the remaining eleven tribes, but no doubt he would have had it not been for the interference of Abner, Saul's captain. Abner established Saul's surviving son, Ishbosheth, as king of the northern tribes, triggering a civil war throughout the land. It was a period of much bloodshed in Israel, marked by cruel assassinations and political intrigue. Ishbosheth's rule was doomed to failure, lasting only two years, while David's popularity continued to mount. Finally, Ishbosheth was murdered, and the northern tribes requested that David become king of the entire nation. David had the unique experience of being anointed king three times—first by Samuel, then by the elders of Judah, and finally by representatives from the nation.

One of the first things David did after his coronation was to drive the Jebusites from their strongholds at Jerusalem and to make it his capital city. As a result, Jerusalem became the political and religious center of the nation. To further secure and solidify his kingdom, David undertook additional military campaigns against the Philistines and the Ammonites and emerged victorious.

As great a man as David was, he was not without faults. The first ten chapters of 2 Samuel tell of his glory, but the last fourteen tell of his sin. The Bible is a Book of Truth and it whitewashes no one's life, including that of kings. In brazen detail the story of David's adulterous relationship with Bathsheba and the subsequent murder of her husband is told. The sordid affair was revealed by the Lord to the prophet Nathan who then confronted David with it through the use of a parable. Nathan's words, "Thou art the man," struck conviction deep within David's heart. Recognizing the terribleness of his sins, he genuinely repented (see Psalms 32 and 51). Though repentant and forgiven, David nonetheless suffered the consequences of his sins. The prophet's words, "The sword shall never depart from thine house," were to haunt him the rest of his days. Within his own family he paid a fourfold penalty for his sins—the death of his child by Bathsheba, the sin of incest between Amnon and Tamar, the murder of Amnon by Absalom, and finally, Absalom's rebellion and tragic death. The tears and grief of a brokenhearted father will forever remind us that sin exacts a heavy toll.

1 KINGS

Author	Date of Writing	Theme	Key Personalities	Main Events
Jeremiah	550 B.C.	Israel's successful kings were those who honored God.	Solomon, Elijah, Ahab, Jezebel	Solomon's Wisdom, Dedication of Solomon's Temple, Visit of Queen of Sheba, Division of Israel, Ministry of Elijah

The two Books of Kings, like the two Books of Samuel, provide a continuing history of Israel. The Book of 1 Kings begins where 2 Samuel ends with a record of the last days of David's reign. It covers a period of approximately 150 years. The purpose of the book was not only to record the history of the kings, but to show that the success of any king (and of the nation as a whole) depended on his allegiance to God's law. Failure in this respect by many, if not most of Israel's monarchs, resulted in the decline of the kingdom and ultimately its collapse.

Shortly before David's death, Solomon was crowned king to prevent a threatened rebellion by Adonijah, another of David's sons. Solomon was the youngest son of David, born to Bathsheba after their legal marriage. He was raised in the finery and luxury of the king's court; consequently, he knew none of the hardships which David had faced in his rise to the throne. Solomon's vain love for material splendor set him on a course to amass one of the greatest fortunes of the then known world. "Solomon in all his glory" was a phrase that characterized his reign, and he is widely known for his wealth, his wives, and his wisdom.

Perhaps the greatest of Solomon's achievements was the construction of the Temple. This was the first permanent center of worship the nation of Israel had. Solomon's Temple was one of the wonders of the ancient world, beautifully ornamented by gold, silver, and precious stones. Thousands of skilled artisans and workmen were required in its construction, and it took a period of seven years to complete. It stood from the time of its dedication about 960 B.C. until it was destroyed by the Babylonian armies of Nebuchadnezzar in 586 B.C., almost four centuries later.

At the death of Solomon, the United Kingdom of Israel came to an end and the nation divided into two kingdoms. The Northern Kingdom was thereafter known as Israel and the Southern Kingdom as Judah. Hostility existed between the two, and the lack of unity left both nations vulnerable to their enemies.

The Book of 1 Kings contains the record of the early history of the divided kingdom. The list of kings for both Israel and Judah often conclude with the tragic words, "He did evil in the sight of the Lord." Except for sporadic outbreaks of revival and renewal, it was a time of great sin and idolatry throughout the land.

One of the bright spots in the Book of 1 Kings is the appearance of the God-fearing prophet Elijah. He entered the scene during the reign of wicked Ahab and Jezebel and denounced their attempts to establish Baal worship in Israel. Clad in a garment of camel's hair with a leather girdle about his waist, this thundering prophet dared to stand against the power of the king and the idolatry of the times and to declare his loyalty to Jehovah. He ultimately challenged Ahab and the prophets of Baal to a contest on Mt. Carmel. After the prophets of Baal failed to get an answer from their god, Elijah prayed a short, simple prayer. God answered by fire from the skies to vindicate Himself as the true God of Israel.

Elijah's ministry was especially honored by God in that many notable miracles were performed among the people. He finally obtained the signal honor of being the second person to be "translated" or taken to heaven without passing through "the valley of the shadow of death."

2 KINGS

Author	Date of Writing	Theme	Key Personalities	Main Events
Jeremiah	550 B.C.	Rejection of God brings judgment.	Elisha, Hezekiah, Josiah	Elisha's Ministry, Kings of Israel, Kings of Judah, Fall of Israel, Fall of Judah

Upon Solomon's death and the accession of his son Rehoboam to the throne, a man named Jeroboam, acting as spokesman for a large segment of the people, appealed for relief from the heavy tax burden Solomon had laid upon them. Unwisely, Rehoboam rejected this appeal and the ten northern tribes rebelled, establishing the kingdom of Israel. They selected Jeroboam as their first king, and he began immediately to lead the people into idolatry by setting up golden calves in Bethel and Dan. The Holy Record sadly refers to him over twenty times as "Jeroboam, the son of Nebat, who made Israel to sin." A total of nineteen kings ruled over Israel during its 250-year history, but the picture never improves. Not one king out of the nineteen was a righteous man; all of them "did evil before the Lord." Having forsaken the God of their fathers and rejecting the message of the prophets, the heavy hand of God's judgment fell upon Israel. In 721 B.C., the cruel and merciless Assyrians from the North swooped down upon them, ravaged the country, and carried many of the people into captivity. With this mass deportation, the ten tribes virtually disappeared from history and the nation of Israel was no more.

The Southern Kingdom of Judah survived 150 years longer than did the Northern Kingdom of Israel. Judah, like Israel, also had nineteen kings (all of whom were from the lineage of David). While Judah's history is also marred by the worship of idols, there were periods of spiritual renewal led by good kings who made a commendable effort to call the people back to God. Among the good kings of Israel were Asa,

35

Jehoshaphat, Joash, Uzziah, Hezekiah, and Josiah. Probably more than any other king, Hezekiah is spoken of in the Scripture as being a godly king. He was a man of strong faith and earnest prayer. His intercession to God was no doubt the reason Judah was not overcome by the Assyrians at the same time the Northern Kingdom fell (2 Kings 19).

Ultimately, however, Judah suffered the same fate as did Israel and for the same reasons (see 2 Chronicles 36:14-21). During the reign of Zedekiah (586 B.C.), the Babylonians invaded the land of Judah, destroyed the Temple, plundered the land, and carried away the choice young men into captivity. The destruction of Jerusalem and the futile plight of the people under the crushing blows of the Babylonian army is one of the saddest events in all history. This nation would not rise again for seventy years until God's prophetic Word was fulfilled.

Perhaps the most colorful personality described in 2 Kings is the prophet Elisha. He stands like a mountain peak above the fog of sin and idolatry of this period. He was Elijah's successor and began his prophetic office when Elijah cast the mantle upon him as he plowed his father's fields.

Known as "the man with a double portion," Elisha performed twice as many miracles as did Elijah, most of which were simple acts of human kindness like those of Jesus. He healed the waters of the spring at Jericho; he predicted the success of an expedition against the Moabites; he increased the widow's oil; he foretold the birth of a son to the childless woman of Shunem and later raised the son to life when he died of a sunstroke; he made safe the pot of poisoned food; he made the borrowed ax head swim. Even after his death, there was so much life in Elisha's bones that when the body of a dead Israelite came into contact with his skeleton the Israelite was restored to life again.

KINGS OF ISRAEL

1. Jeroboam	19 years	1 Kings	12:20
2. Nadab	2 years	1 Kings	12:25
3. Baasha	24 years	1 Kings	15:33
4. Elah	2 years	1 Kings	16:8
5. Zimri	7 years	1 Kings	16:10
6. Omri	12 years	1 Kings	16:23
7. Ahab	22 years	1 Kings	16:29
8. Ahaziah	2 years	1 Kings	22:51
9. Jehoram	12 years	2 Kings	3:1
10. Jehu	28 years	2 Kings	9:13
11. Jehoahaz	17 years	2 Kings	13:1
12. Jehoash (Joash)	16 years	2 Kings	13:10
13. Jeroboam	41 years	2 Kings	14:23
14. Zachariah	6 months	2 Kings	15:8
15. Shallum	1 month	2 Kings	15:13
16. Menahem	10 years	2 Kings	15:17
17. Pekahiah	2 years	2 Kings	15:23
18. Pekah	20 years	2 Kings	15:27
19. Hoshea	9 years	2 Kings	17:1

KINGS OF JUDAH

1. Rehoboam	17 years	1 Kings	12:17
2. Abijam	3 years	1 Kings	15:1
3. Asa	41 years	1 Kings	15:9
4. Jehoshaphat	25 years	1 Kings	15:24
5. Jehoram	8 years	2 Kings	8:16
6. Ahaziah	1 year	2 Kings	8:25
7. Jehoash (Joash)	40 years	2 Kings	12:1
8. Amaziah	29 years	2 Kings	14:1
9. Azariah (Uzziah)	52 years	2 Kings	15:1
10. Jotham	16 years	2 Kings	15:32
11. Ahaz	16 years	2 Kings	16:1
12. Hezekiah	29 years	2 Kings	18:1
13. Manasseh	55 years	2 Kings	21:1
14. Amon	2 years	2 Kings	29:19
15. Josiah	31 years	2 Kings	22:1
16. Jehoahaz	3 months	2 Kings	23:31
17. Jehoiakim	11 years	2 Kings	23:36
18. Jehoiachin	3 months	2 Kings	24:8
19. Zedekiah	11 years	2 Kings	24:18

1 AND 2 CHRONICLES

Author	Date of Writing	Theme	Key Personalities	Main Events
Ezra	450-425 B.C.	The Rich Heritage of Israel and Their Covenant Relationship to God	David, Solomon, Other Kings of Judah	David's Preparation for Building the Temple, Dedication of the Temple, Queen of Sheba's Visit to Solomon, Genealogy of David's Lineage

Like Samuel and Kings, the Books of Chronicles were originally one book. This single book was divided into two by the translation of the Septuagint (the early Greek translation of the Scriptures). In the Septuagint, the Chronicles are referred to as *paralipomena* which means "things omitted." Thus, the Chronicles are understood to be a supplement to the Books of Kings.

Ezra, the noted scribe and priest who led a group of exiles back to Palestine in 458 B.C., is generally regarded as the author of the Chronicles. To reclaim lost land and to restore the worship of God, Ezra felt that the returning captives must be made aware of their previous laws, their ancestral heritage, and their national leadership. While the Chronicles appear to be a repetition of the events recorded in 2 Samuel and the Books of Kings, there is a significant difference in that the historical action is seen through the eyes of a priest. Emphasis is placed upon the religious rather than the political aspects. Ezra intentionally omitted detailed activities of the kings and prophets, stressing instead the rich heritage of the people and their covenant relationship to God.

The Book of 1 Chronicles is a "miniature Old Testament," tracing in capsule form the flow of Old Testament history from Adam to the Babylonian captivity and Cyrus' decree allowing the exiled Jews to return home. The book is heavy with genealogies and focuses almost entirely on the reigns of King David and his son Solomon.

The Book of 2 Chronicles is the continuing history of the Southern Kingdom of Judah from Solomon's time to the period of captivity. The Northern Kingdom of Israel is given little attention since only the Davidic line was regarded as representing true Israel.

The more prominent passages in 1 Chronicles are God's covenant with David (17:11-14) and David's beautiful prayer of praise (29:10-19). The significant passages of 2 Chronicles are Solomon's prayer for wisdom (1:7-12), the dedication of Solomon's Temple (chapters 5-7), the visit of the queen of Sheba (9:1-12), and the prediction of the length of the captivity (36:20-21).

A choice selection for memorization is 2 Chronicles 7:14—"If my people, which are called by my name, shall humble themselves, and pray, and seek my face, and turn from their wicked ways; then will I hear from heaven, and will forgive their sin, and will heal their land." Another is 2 Chronicles 16:9—"For the eyes of the Lord run to and fro throughout the whole earth, to shew himself strong in the behalf of them whose heart is perfect toward him."

EZRA

Author	Date of Writing	Theme	Key Personalities	Main Events
Ezra	456-444 B.C.	Return of the Jews From Captivity	Zerubbabel, Cyrus—King of Persia, Ezra	Return of Exiles With Zerubbabel, Construction of Zerubbabel's Temple, Return of Ezra

Ezra takes its name from its principle character, and although not specifically identified in the book as its author, he is generally thought to be. The Book of Ezra along with the Books of Nehemiah and Chronicles originally formed one book.

Ezra is the record of the fulfillment of God's promise to restore Israel to her land after the seventy years of captivity in Babylon (Jeremiah 25:11). The Persian king, Cyrus, conquered the Babylonian empire in 539 B.C. One year later he issued a proclamation permitting the Jews to return to their homeland. Ezra 1:1 states that "the Lord stirred up the spirit of Cyrus," causing him to take this course of action.

The Book of Ezra may be subdivided in two parts since it concerns itself with two separate groups of exiles who returned to Palestine—the first led by Zerubbabel (chapters 1-6) and the second under Ezra some eighty years later (chapters 7-10).

Approximately fifty years elapsed between the destruction of Jerusalem and the return of the first group of exiles under Zerubbabel and Jeshua. This group numbered about fifty thousand. Upon arrival in Jerusalem, their first objective was to restore the worship of Jehovah by building an altar for the daily sacrifices. This was followed by an all-out effort to rebuild the Temple which had been destroyed earlier by Nebuchadnezzar's army. When the Temple foundation was laid, the event was celebrated by the blowing of trumpets, the clanging of cymbals, and the singing of psalms.

For the younger generation, it was a time of great rejoicing. But for the older people who had seen the greater splendor of Solomon's Temple, it was a time of sad reflection and weeping (Ezra 3:13). The "second temple" (or Zerubbabel's Temple, as it came to be known) was not completed until approximately twenty years later—the work being halted by hostile Samaritans and other enemies who convinced the king of Persia (then Artaxerxes) that the completion of the Temple would promote rebellion in Jerusalem and Judaea.

Fifty years after the completion of the Temple, the scribe Ezra received permission from Artaxerxes, or Ahasuerus, to lead a second contingency back to Jerusalem. This group consisted of 1,500 men along with members of their families. The journey from Babylon to Jerusalem was an arduous and dangerous one, requiring four months to complete. Before leaving, Ezra proclaimed a fast for the success of his venture. His strong faith gave him calm assurance that God was with him. In fact, he had so assured the king that God would protect their mission that he was ashamed to request an armed escort (Ezra 8:22).

Upon arrival in Jerusalem, Ezra was grieved to find that the people had departed from the law of God and had intermarried with the Gentiles, adopting their pagan practices. Ezra set about to initiate religious reform enforcing a plan of separation upon all who had married foreign wives (Ezra 10). His deep concern for national repentance and a return to the worship of Jehovah is reflected in his prayer, "O my God, I am ashamed and blush to lift up my face to thee, my God: for our iniquities are increased over our head, and our trespass is grown up unto the heavens" (Ezra 9:6). Ezra's leadership prompted a sincere response on the part of the people and resulted in spiritual revival throughout Israel.

NEHEMIAH

Author	Date of Writing	Theme	Key Personalities	Main Events
Nehemiah	445-425 B.C.	Success is achieved through vision, planning, and diligent labor.	Nehemiah, Sanballet, Tobiah, Geshem	Nehemiah in the Court of Artaxerxes, Rebuilding the Walls of Jerusalem, Nehemiah's Reforms as Governor of Judah

The Book of Nehemiah is generally regarded as the auto-biography of the man for whom the book is named. Nehemiah is one of the few Jews of dispersion to achieve a prominent position in the Persian kingdom. Appointed as cup-bearer to King Artaxerxes I, he became a trusted servant and advisor and was to some extent responsible for the security of the king. One of his chief functions as cup-bearer was to certify that the wine the king drank contained no poison. This high office also placed him among a limited number of court officials who could be admitted to the king while the queen was present.

While serving the king at his royal winter palace in Shushan, Nehemiah received heartbreaking news from Jerusalem that the gates and walls of the city were still unrepaired, the Temple services were being neglected, and the Jewish remnant was suffering reproach and affliction. So distressed was Nehemiah by this report that his weeping, accompanied by prayer and fasting for God's intervention, continued for days.

King Artaxerxes observed Nehemiah's sad countenance and upon learning the reasons, granted him permission to go to Jerusalem to correct the situation. The king also appointed Nehemiah governor of Judah, gave him letters of commendation to other governors along the way, and provided him with a cavalry escort.

Upon arrival in Jerusalem, Nehemiah made inspection of the city walls and set about to accomplish his mission. He successfully rallied the people to assist with the work but was severely opposed by neighboring enemies—notably Sanballet, the Samaritan; Tobiah, the Ammonite; and Geshem, the Arabian. Nevertheless, in spite of ridicule (4:3), armed attack (4:8), physical threats (4:11), and deceptive requests for negotiation (6:2-4), the persistent Nehemiah and his workmen completed the mammoth project in only fifty-two days. Often compelled to work with sword in one hand and trowel in the other, Nehemiah reflected a dogged determination that has been a source of inspiration for centuries to the would-be fainthearted. Few men in Bible history have demonstrated greater leadership ability, organizational skill, and personal integrity than did Nehemiah. He is remembered as a man of courage, faith, and action, and he takes rank among Israel's noblest patriots. His name means "consolation of the Lord" or "Jehovah comforts."

Nehemiah served as governor of Judah for twelve years after which he returned briefly to Artaxerxes' court (1:1, 13:6). He then returned to Judah where he called the people to repentance.

ESTHER

Author	Date of Writing	Theme	Key Personalities	Main Events
Uncertain	465 B.C.	God controls all events.	Esther, Mordecai, Ahasuerus (Xerxes), Haman	Divorce of Queen Vashti, Esther Becomes Queen of Persia, Haman's Plan to Exterminate the Jews, God's Deliverance Through Esther, Feast of Purim

Esther is the last of the historical books of the Old Testament and the second book of the Bible to be named for a woman (the other is Ruth). It is not a part of the mainstream of Hebrew history, but provides instead an interesting sidelight into the conditions prevailing among the Jews who chose to remain in the land of Persia. The events took place at about the same time Nehemiah and Ezra were in Jerusalem attempting to reestablish their homeland. The Book of Esther is sometimes criticized because the name of God is not mentioned. However, no book in the Bible demonstrates more beautifully the providential watchfulness of God over His chosen people than does Esther. As Matthew Henry, the renowned Bible commentator, states, "If the name of God is not here, His finger is."

The story of Esther unfolds in the courts of Persia during the reign of King Ahasuerus, known as Xerxes in secular history. After dethroning Queen Vashti for refusing to exhibit herself before a party of drunken princes, the king began a search for her successor. A beautiful young Hebrew girl named Hadassah (or Esther) was selected from among all the maidens of the kingdom to be the new queen. Esther was orphaned as a small child and was brought up by her older cousin, Mordecai. Mordecai was an official in the king's court and gained considerable favor with Ahasuerus by revealing a secret plot against the king's life.

However, serious trouble erupted when he incurred the

wrath of Haman, a powerful and ambitious courtier of the king. When Mordecai refused to bow before the arrogant Haman, his hatred rose to a boiling point. Through devious manipulation, Haman succeeded in persuading the king to approve an evil scheme which would have exterminated the Jewish population in a single day. Mordecai appealed swiftly to Queen Esther for help, suggesting that the providence of God had made her queen of Persia for the purpose of preserving the Jewish race. His words, "Who knoweth whether thou art come to the kingdom for such a time as this" (4:14), gave Esther courage to approach the king even though doing so without invitation placed her own life in jeopardy. In accordance with her predetermined plan, Esther invited Ahasuerus and Haman to a banquet where she revealed Haman's scheme to the king. Upon learning of Haman's deception, Ahasuerus was furious and commanded that Haman be hanged on the same gallows he had prepared for Mordecai. A law of the "Medes and Persians" could not be revoked; therefore, Ahasuerus issued a supplementary edict permitting the Jews to arm themselves against attack. God's marvelous intervention for the Jews on this occasion prompted great celebration and resulted in many Persians being converted to the Jewish faith (8:17). In connection with this celebration, Mordecai instituted a joyful spiritual feast which he called the "Feast of Purim"—Purim being taken from the word *pur* referring to the lots Haman cast to decide the day the Jews would be slain.

Queen Esther, whose name means "a star," is regarded as a heroine of the Jewish people. She was a lady of both charm and courage and without doubt was an instrument of divine grace to preserve the race through which the Savior of the world was to come.

REVIEW — UNIT 2

(Joshua — Esther)

1. Name the twelve historical books.
2. Who was Moses' successor?
3. List five of the judges of Israel.
4. Name the three kings of the United Kingdom of Israel.
5. Discuss briefly the key events in the life of the prophet Elijah.
6. Outline the factors which led to the division of the United Kingdom into two separate nations.
7. What happened to the ten Jewish tribes that were carried away into Assyria?
8. What was "Zerubbabel's Temple"?
9. List several miracles performed by the prophet Elisha.
10. Identify the following:

Rahab	Samuel	Jonathan	Haman
Ruth	Saul	Ishbosheth	Mordecai
Boaz	Jesse	Abner	Nehemiah
Eli	Hannah	Bathsheba	Hadassah
Baal	Chemosh	Purim	Ezra

Fill in the Blank:

1. _____'s name means "Jehovah is salvation."
2. The Historical Books cover approximately _____ years of Hebrew history.
3. Rahab became the wife of _____.
4. _____ and _____ are perhaps the most colorful and best known of all the judges.
5. _____ and _____ are two books of the Bible named for women.
6. The _____ is an early Greek translation of the Scriptures.

47

7. _____ was dedicated by his mother to the Lord at a young age and was trained by Eli the priest.

8. Saul was the son of _____ and became the first king of Israel.

9. Saul's three sons were _____, _____, and _____.

10. The reign of David is known as the _____ of Israel's history.

11. It was the prophet _____ who confronted David with his sins.

12. _____ is known for his wealth, his wives, and his wisdom.

13. Elijah's prophetic ministry took place during the reign of _____ and _____.

14. The nation of Israel was defeated by the _____; the nation of Judah was defeated by the _____.

15. Two separate groups of exiles returned to Palestine, the first led by _____, the second some eighty years later under _____.

16. Nehemiah occupied the position of _____ to the Persian king Artaxerxes I.

17. The name of God is not mentioned in the Book of _____.

18. _____ is referred to as the priest judge; _____ is referred to as the prophet judge.

19. _____ was the great-grandmother of David.

20. _____'s name means "a star."

UNIT 3

JOB

Author	Date of Writing	Theme	Key Personalities	Main Events
Uncertain— Possibilities: Job himself, Elihu, Moses, Solomon	Uncertain	Why do the righteous suffer?	Job, Eliphaz, Bildad, Zophar, Elihu	Job's Suffering and Triumph

The third major division of the Old Testament is composed of five important books known as the poetical and wisdom books: Job, Psalms, Proverbs, Ecclesiastes, and the Song of Solomon. These books differ from the historical books in that they are devotional in content rather than historical and deal with the inner experience of the individual rather than the outward development of a nation. They set forth the deepest longings and aspirations of the human heart to know God, and they seek to identify the means by which a right relationship can be established with Him.

Found in the poetical and wisdom books are three basic types of Hebrew poetry: lyric, didactic, and dramatic. Lyric (or song type) poetry had its beginning before Moses, but it reached its apex in the Psalms of David—the "sweet psalmist of Israel" (2 Samuel 23:1). The didactic (or teaching) type of poetry is found in Proverbs and Ecclesiastes. The dramatic type of poetry is found in Job and perhaps in the Song of Solomon. In the dramatic books, the action

49

is reflected in the movement of ideas rather than in persons and events.

The Book of Job, the first of the poetical books, is regarded by many as one of the greatest literary works of all times. As was said of Goliath's sword, "There is none like it." Tennyson called it "the greatest poem, whether of ancient or modern literature." The events of the book probably took place near the time of the patriarch Abraham. Its central personality is a man named Job, whose very life became a testing ground to prove the purity of his motives for serving God.

Satan's sneer, "Doth Job fear God for nought?" (Job 1:9), could not go unchallenged by God. He, therefore, permitted Satan to launch an all-out attack upon Job as a test of his faithfulness. Almost overnight Job was reduced from riches to rags. Sabeans stole his oxen, lightning killed his sheep, Chaldeans drove off his camels, and a whirlwind killed his sons. As if that were not enough, Satan heaped misery upon misery by afflicting Job with a horrible disease of boils from which he received no relief except by scraping himself with pieces of broken pottery. So distraught was his wife from the avalanche of misfortune that she suggested that he "curse God, and die" (Job 2:9). To die Job was willing, but to curse God and renounce his faith was (as far as he was concerned) an eternal impossibility. His anguished but trusting cry, "Though he slay me, yet will I trust in him" (Job 13:15), reflected admirable devotion to God and persistent strength of character, despite the worst of circumstances. Job's beautiful example of patience in suffering and the ultimate triumph of his faith have been the means of bringing hope and calm assurance to the hearts of thousands who have themselves walked the lonely ravines of pain, death, and personal loss.

Since the primary objective of the Book of Job is to deal with the age-old question, "Why do the righteous suffer?" there are several important lessons to be remembered:

1. The purpose of human suffering is not always evident to the sufferer or to those who look on.

2. Suffering may benefit the sufferer, transforming his character into "pure gold."

3. The problem of suffering cannot be totally resolved within the limits of this life. It must be viewed in the light of the compensations of eternity.

4. Perfection of moral character is compatible with misunderstanding, suspicion, ill health, poverty, and partial light. Job was "perfect and upright" (Job 1:1) before the Lord and yet experienced all of the above.

5. The suffering of God's saints proves the sustaining grace of God.

PSALMS

Author	Date of Writing	Theme	Key Personalities	Main Events
Various Authors: David, Solomon, Sons of Korah, Asaph, Others	Various dates— Most were written during the time of David and Solomon (10th century B.C.).	Prayer, Praise, and Worship	God—The Object of Man's Worship	

One of the most beautiful and perhaps most loved portions of Scripture is the Book of Psalms. It is a book of rare devotional quality, and its inspired passages have made it as timeless as eternity itself.

The Book of Psalms has often been referred to as the "Hymnbook of the Ages." The early Christian fathers called it the "psalter" while the Jews identified it as the "Book of Praises." The term *psalm* comes from the Greek (Septuagint translation) and originally meant "songs accompanied by stringed instruments." It is basically a collection of 150 poems which were apparently set to music in Bible days and formed a significant part of Hebrew worship.

Seventy-three of the Psalms were written by David; twelve are credited to Asaph (David's choir director); eleven are ascribed to the sons of Korah (a noted group of singers during David's time). Jeduthun wrote three; Solomon is credited with two (Psalms 72 and 127); Ethan wrote one and Heman one (Psalm 80). Psalm 90 is credited to Moses. Fifty of the Psalms are known as "orphan" psalms; that is, the name of the composer is not known.

The Book of Psalms is subdivided into five books (or five separate collections of songs), each ending with a magnificent doxology of praise to God. These doxologies are found at the conclusion of Psalms 41, 72, 89, 106, and 150. The Psalms begin with a beatitude, as does the Sermon on the Mount, and gradually crescendo to an exultant acclamation of praise in a group of songs known as the "Hallelujah Psalms" (146-150).

Following is a list of the several different types of Psalms found in this ancient hymnal:

Psalms of Praise (8, 19, 34, 54)

Psalms of Meditation and Reflection (1, 15, 23, 121)

Liturgical Psalms (those composed for and used during special services of the sanctuary—113-118)

Psalms of Penitence and Supplication (3, 4, 5, 6, 38, 51)

Psalms of Thanksgiving (100, 103, 116)

Historical Psalms (78, 106, 108)

Of particular importance are the prophetic or messianic psalms. These are poems that find their truest fulfillment in the person and ministry of Jesus Christ. Hundreds of years before His birth many of the details of Christ's life were told with amazing accuracy. His anointing by God's Spirit (Psalm 45:6-8), His prayer in the garden (Psalm 40:7, 8), the piercing of His hands and feet (Psalm 22:16), the gambling of the soldiers for His raiment (Psalm 22:18), His cry of distress on the cross (Psalm 22:1), and His resurrection (Psalms 16:10).

The Psalms teach us to sing and to worship. They encourage us to respond to God's boundless blessings with praise and thanksgiving. They contribute to the development of positive attitudes about life and inspire qualities of faith, hope, and courage. Whether in joyful anthems of worship or in deep reflection upon His goodness, the Psalms allow us to turn quietly away from ourselves to Him whose peace, presence, and power are abundantly adequate for all life's needs. What a refreshing experience!

PROVERBS

Author	Date of Writing	Theme	Key Personalities	Main Events
Solomon and Others	950-700 B.C.	Wisdom for Living		

A proverb is a brief, pointed saying or maxim expressing a specific truth or fact. Popularized by time and common usage, it is usually moralistic in nature, highly practical, and easy to remember and quote.

As the Book of Psalms is a collection of Hebrew hymns, so the Book of Proverbs is a collection of Hebrew wisdom. Together with the Books of Job and Ecclesiastes, the Proverbs form what has come to be appreciated as the world's greatest library of wisdom. Unlike other wisdom collections, the Proverbs are not to be regarded as mere reflections or observations of an astute mind, but rather as divine principles applied and tested in the school of human experience. These principles find their rootage deep in the Word of God and establish an unequalled code of ethics and morality which has guided human conduct for centuries.

The keynote or foundational theme of the book is Proverbs 9:10—"The fear of the Lord is the beginning of wisdom"—repeated in various forms throughout the Proverbs (1:7, 29; 10:27; 15:33; 19:23). This captivating theme strongly reminds us that respect for God and submission to His will are the very fountainhead from which all wisdom springs. To obey God and keep His commandments is the highest wisdom and the secret of true and lasting happiness.

The Proverbs touch almost every conceivable aspect of life (family, friends, business relationships) and cover a wide variety of subjects including wealth, poverty, sin, righteousness, pride, humility, justice, vengeance, gluttony, love, lust, laziness, honesty, helpfulness, training of children, control of the tongue, and common sense.

Solomon is credited as the author of most of the Proverbs with the exception of chapter 30, written by Agur, and chapter 31, written by Lemuel. According to 1 Kings 4:32, Solomon wrote a total of 1,005 songs and 3,000 Proverbs which unfortunately means that all of his works have not been preserved. The Book of Proverbs probably represents the cream of his writings.

Found in Proverbs 3:5, 6 is Solomon's threefold rule of life: "Trust in the Lord with all thine heart; and lean not unto thine own understanding. In all thy ways acknowledge him, and he shall direct thy paths." Another noteworthy passage is the beautiful tribute to virtuous womanhood given in chapter 31.

ECCLESIASTES

Author	Date of Writing	Theme	Key Personalities	Main Events
Solomon	935 B.C.	A personal relationship with God is the only means of true and lasting happiness.		

The title of this book in Hebrew is *Koheleth*, which means "one who speaks at an assembly." It also means "an ecclesiastic" or "preacher." The word *preacher* appears seven times throughout the book and is used in reference to the speaker or writer (1:1, 2, 12; 7:27; 12:8, 9, 10).

To understand the true message of Ecclesiastes, the book must be considered as a whole and not in isolated fragments. Indeed, without the writer's final conclusion in the last chapter, portions of the book would appear to give credence to false ideologies, such as materialism (2:7-10), fatalism (3:1-15), and deism (3:1; 4:16).

Ecclesiastes may be regarded as the reflections and experiences of a man (probably Solomon) whose mind was in deep conflict over the basic issues of life. His deepest yearnings, like those of every human being, were to achieve happiness and to discover life's true meaning. Unfortunately, the pursuit of these goals led him in every direction but the right one. He studied the sciences (1:5-7), explored human reasoning (1:13), traveled the roads of carnal pleasure (2:1-3), dedicated himself to a variety of work projects (2:4), planted gardens, vineyards, and orchards (2:4), amassed a fortune (2:7, 8), and even tried music as a means of soothing his troubled heart (2:8). The expression "under the sun," used twenty times in this book, suggests that Solomon became totally given over to worldly philosophy and worldly pursuits. His restless, prodigal spirit so dominated his character that he openly confessed, "Whatsoever mine eyes desired I kept not from them, I withheld not my heart from any joy" (2:10).

The tragedy of such a philosophy (as Solomon finally discovered) is that it is based solely upon earthly values. The little satisfaction and contentment it affords are but temporary and incomplete. Solomon saw earthly life at its best, explored its every pleasure, and enjoyed its richest honors. But in the end his heart was overwhelmed by the emptiness of it all. The degree of his disillusionment and frustration is summed up in the oft-repeated phrase, "All was vanity and vexation of spirit" (2:11).

Toward the conclusion of the book, Solomon slowly began to emerge from his doubts and confusion, becoming convinced that a right relationship with God is the only avenue to lasting happiness. In chapter 12 he urged youth to not make the same mistakes he made but instead to remember God in their tender and productive years (12:1). Finally, out of the woods in his thinking, Solomon invited everyone to hear the conclusion of his lifelong search—"Let us hear the conclusion of the whole matter: Fear God, and keep his commandments: for this is the whole duty of man. For God shall bring every work into judgment, with every secret thing, whether it be good, or whether it be evil" (12:13, 14).

THE SONG OF SOLOMON

Author	Date of Writing	Theme	Key Personalities	Main Events
Solomon	965 B.C.	The Beauty of Wedded Love		

The Song of Solomon is a tender and expressive love song, extolling the beauty and joys of wedded love. It has often been criticized for its intimacies. However, when viewed in proper context, it becomes acceptable both in terms of the social customs of the times and in its support of the rightful place of physical love within the bounds of marriage.

From a historical perspective, the Song of Solomon is the story of the courtship and marriage of the great King Solomon to a humble but beautiful maiden, whose daily chores consisted of tending the family vineyard. Identified only as a Shulamite (a resident of Shulem or Shunem), the dream of this suntanned country girl suddenly turned to reality when not a prince but the king himself wooed her and won her hand in marriage.

The song progresses with vivid description of the king's love for his young bride and of her mutual love for him. Abounding in metaphors and set in the Oriental imagery of blossoming springtime, this captivating song tells the beauty of their shared love.

"Love is strong as death. . . . Many waters cannot quench love, neither can the floods drown it: if a man would give all the substance of his house for love, it would utterly be contemned" (8:6, 7).

The kind of qualitative love described in the Song of Solomon has strength of character, leaps every barrier, is enduring, and cannot be bought at any price. It is reminiscent of Saint Paul's wonderful classic on the same subject where he affirms, "Love never faileth" (see 1 Corinthians 13:8). Some interpreters see in the love of an earthly king for a maid of lowly birth a type or picture of the love of God for His chosen people. The Jews apparently subscribed to this interpretation, for in the *Talmud* (a collection of Jewish civil and religious laws), the "beloved" is understood to be God, and the "bride" is represented as the congregation of Israel. The Song of Solomon was often read at the feast of the Passover in remembrance of Jehovah's great love for Israel.

In the New Testament the comparison of Christ to the bridegroom and His Church to the bride is a very familiar and beautiful analogy (Ephesians 5:22-32). Among Christians the love expressions of the Song of Solomon have been commonly regarded as the tender entreaties of Christ who "loved the church, and gave himself for it" (Ephesians 5:25).

The title "song of songs" (1:1) seems to indicate that Solomon regarded this composition to be the choicest of the 1,005 songs (1 Kings 4:32) which he wrote during his lifetime. It reveals much about the personality, character, and interests of the writer and quite possibly reflects the only pure romance he ever had. By any standard of measurement, the "song of songs" must be regarded as a superb work.

REVIEW — UNIT 3

(Job—Song of Solomon)

1. Name the five poetical and wisdom books.
2. Give three types of Hebrew poetry.
3. Who is known as "the sweet psalmist of Israel"?
4. Job is an example of the _____ type of poetry.
5. Psalms is an example of the _____ type of poetry.
6. Proverbs is an example of the _____ type of poetry.
7. Taking into account the experiences of Job, discuss briefly the question, "Why do the righteous suffer?"
8. What book is called the "hymnbook of the ages"?
9. Twelve of the psalms are credited to _____.
10. Psalms 146-150 are known as the _____.
11. Tell why the prophetic or messianic psalms are of particular importance to the Christian.
12. As the Book of _____ is a collection of Hebrew hymns, so the Book of _____ is a collection of Hebrew wisdom.
13. _____ is credited as the author of most of the Proverbs with the exception of chapter 30, written by _____, and chapter 31, written by _____.
14. Solomon wrote a total of _____ songs and _____ proverbs.
15. Chapter 31 of Proverbs gives a beautiful tribute to _____.
16. The title of _____ in Hebrew is *Koheleth* which means _____.
17. The word _____ is used seven times in Ecclesiastes.
18. Solomon's frustration and disappointment with life is summed up in the phrase "All was _____ and vexation of the _____."
19. Memorize Ecclesiastes 12:13, 14.
20. The theme of the Song of Solomon is _____.
21. Solomon called his song _____.

UNIT 4

ISAIAH

Author	Date of Writing	Theme	Key Personalities	Main Events
Isaiah	740-680 B.C.	Judgment (chapters 1-39), Redemption (chapters 40-66)	Isaiah, Hezekiah, Other kings	Prophecies Against Israel and Judah; Prophecies of Judgments Against Various Nations; Prophecies Concerning the Future Messiah

The fourth major division of the Old Testament is known as "the prophets" and includes the Books of Isaiah through Malachi. Seventeen in number, the prophetical books may be classified as follows:

Major Prophets

Isaiah
Jeremiah
(Lamentations)
Ezekiel
Daniel

Minor Prophets

Hosea	Jonah	Zephaniah
Joel	Micah	Haggai
Amos	Nahum	Zechariah
Obadiah	Habakkuk	Malachi

The period of the prophets extends from the ninth century B.C. to the fifth century B.C., a period of some four hundred years. This era in the history of the Hebrew people was marked by moral, spiritual, and political failure and ultimately witnessed the overthrow of Israel by the Assyrians (721 B.C.) and of Judah by the Babylonians (586 B.C.). The prophets whom God raised up during this dark time were men of sterling character who called for national repentance and made valiant efforts to stem the tide of idolatry and spiritual indifference. However, their pleas and warnings for the most part went unheeded, resulting in the judgments of God upon the people.

Isaiah is considered by many to be the greatest of the prophets of this period. His prophecies spanned the reigns of at least four kings of Judah—Uzziah, Jotham, Ahaz, and Hezekiah—and covered a period of approximately sixty years (740-680 B.C.). Isaiah is believed to have been of royal descent, perhaps a cousin to King Uzziah. It is quite evident from his writings that he had easy access to the royal court (7:3; 37:21; 38:1; 39:3-8) and exercised a powerful influence upon the monarchs of his day.

While Isaiah's ministry was concerned primarily with Judah and Jerusalem (1:1), it was by no means limited thereto. He announced God's impending judgments upon Babylon, Assyria, Egypt, and Israel as well as other surrounding nations.

The Book of Isaiah is a miniature Bible in structure. It contains sixty-six chapters with two major divisions—the first of which contains thirty-nine chapters, the second twenty-seven. The theme of the first section (chapters 1-39) is "judgment" with the prophet announcing the doom of the nations for their sins. The theme of the second part (chapters 40-66) is "redemption," which foretells the return of Judah from captivity and joyfully proclaims the coming of a future Redeemer. Due to its message of hope and comfort, the second half has sometimes been referred to as the "Book of Consolation."

Isaiah is best known to the Christian world for his prophecies concerning the person, work, and kingdom of the Messiah. It is a thrilling testimony to the accuracy of Bible prophecy that seven hundred years before the birth of Christ, Isaiah predicted His virgin birth (7:14), His deity and eternal kingdom (9:1-7), His descent from David (11:1), His vicarious sufferings and death (52:13, 53:12), and His millennial kingdom (chapters 2, 11, 12, 24-27, 59-66). Chapter 53 is the crown jewel in the treasury of the Old Testament, providing a stirring prophetic view of the suffering Savior.

The key word in the Book of Isaiah is *salvation*, which is used at least twenty-eight times throughout the book (12: 3; 25:9; 26:1; 45:17; 49:8; 59:16, 17; 61:10; 62:1). It is also interesting to observe that Isaiah's name means "salvation of Jehovah," which perhaps suggests something of the prophet's message and ministry. According to ancient Jewish tradition, Isaiah was martyred by being placed into the trunk of a hollow tree which was then sawed in half (Hebrews 11:37).

JEREMIAH

Author	Date of Writing	Theme	Key Personalities	Main Events
Jeremiah	627-585 B.C.	Judah's Final Call to Repentance	Jeremiah, Kings of Judah, Nebuchadnezzar, King of Babylon	Jeremiah's Calling, Prophecies Concerning Jerusalem and Judah, Prophecies Regarding Foreign Powers

Jeremiah lived approximately one hundred years after the prophet Isaiah and was the last of the preexilic prophets. His ministry spanned nearly half a century and included the reigns of Kings Josiah, Jehoahaz, Jehoikim, Jehoiachin, and Zedekiah.

Jeremiah came from the little village of Anathoth located about three miles north of Jerusalem. He is identified as the son of Hilkiah the priest. This is perhaps the same Hilkiah referred to in 2 Kings 22 who brought the Book of the Law to the attention of King Josiah, sparking a religious awakening throughout the nation. Jeremiah was called to the prophetic office at a very young age. Reluctant at first to accept the calling, he pleaded that youth, inexperience, and lack of eloquence disqualified him from service (1:6, 7). However, after assurance of divine leadership for his mission, he proclaimed God's message with unswerving loyalty.

At the time of Jeremiah's prophecies, three major powers were vying for world supremacy—Assyria, Babylon, and Egypt. Assyria had ruthlessly ruled the world for three hundred years but was growing weak. Babylon was becoming powerful. Egypt, which had been a world power a thousand years before, was again becoming ambitious with hopes of regaining her lost position. Twenty years before the conflict was settled, the prophet Jeremiah insisted that Babylon would emerge the victor. In 612 B.C., the Assyrian capital of Nineveh fell before the crush of the Babylonian army. And in 605 B.C., the fatal blow was delivered to the Egyptians at the famous Battle of Carchemish. For seventy years Babylon was the undisputed master of the world (25: 11).

Not only did Jeremiah correctly forecast the outcome of the three-way political struggle, but he foresaw Babylon as the weapon of judgment God would use to punish Judah for her sin. Jeremiah's hope was that national repentance would somehow avert the impending disaster, but his pleas for a return to God fell on deaf ears. The word *backslider*, used thirteen times in the Book of Jeremiah, aptly describes the rebellious attitude of the people during this tragic era of Jewish history. Not only was Jeremiah's message rejected, but his prophecy that Babylon would overthrow Judah was regarded as treason. Consequently, he was severely persecuted by his own countrymen. His writings were cut up and burned by King Jehoikim, he was beaten, he received numerous threats on his life, and he suffered arrest and imprisonment on several occasions (11:18-23; 12:6; 18:18; 20:1-3; 26:1-24; 37:11-38:28). Nevertheless, his prophetic utterances came to pass. After the conquest of Assyria and Egypt, Nebuchadnezzar turned his fury upon Judah, partially destroying Jerusalem in 606 B.C. He further devastated it in 597 B.C. and finally burned it and left it in rubble (586 B.C.). When the forces of Nebuchadnezzar took Jerusalem, they were given specific orders to protect Jeremiah. He was freed from prison and given the choice to either go to Babylon or stay in Jerusalem. He chose to remain in Jerusalem. However, within a short period of time, a fanatical band of Jews assassinated Gedaliah (whom Nebuchadnezzar had set up as governor), captured Jeremiah, and fled into Egypt. It is believed that Jeremiah died while in Egypt.

In view of the sad events witnessed by Jeremiah during his lifetime, it isn't surprising that he became known as the "weeping prophet." Although directed of God to deliver a stern message of judgment, he nevertheless was a sensitive and sympathetic man. His messages are filled with impassioned pleas for his people and are saturated with tears for their salvation. He, like the Savior, died of a broken heart, despised and rejected by those he sought to help.

LAMENTATIONS

Author	Date of Writing	Theme	Key Personalities	Main Events
Jeremiah	586-585 B.C.	The Tragedy of Jerusalem's Downfall	Jeremiah	Destruction of Jerusalem

The Book of Lamentations is Jeremiah's funeral dirge over the destruction of Jerusalem by the Babylonian Army in 586 B.C. Without doubt, it is the saddest book in the Bible and has been described as a "hymn of sorrow, every letter written with a tear, every word with the sound of a broken heart" *(Halley's Handbook)*.

Viewing the smoldering ruins of a once proud city, Jeremiah was overcome with inconsolable grief and penned the series of laments or poems which now comprise the Book of Lamentations.

The book was probably written during the short interval between the burning of Jerusalem and Jeremiah's abduction to Egypt (Jeremiah 43:8, 9). With the events still fresh upon his mind and stunned by the unspeakable horrors of the Babylonian conquest, Jeremiah graphically poured out the anguish of his soul. He spared no detail in describing the awful atrocities identified with the Babylonian siege—the rape of the women of Judah by their captors (5:11), the cries of starving children (2:11, 12, 19; 4:4), women boiling their own babies for food (2:20; 4:10), massacre of both men and women by the merciless invaders (2:21), the homeless sleeping in the street (2:21), and the maiming and execution of national leaders (5:12).

It was a sad plight indeed to witness the death throes of a nation and to watch helplessly as friends and kinsmen, chained like animals, were carried away into slavery, their faces to never again be seen.

Jeremiah's grief was further compounded by the gnawing realization that it was the sins of the people which had brought about this catastrophic situation (1:5, 8, 9, 14, 18, 20, 22). The seeds of rebellion against God and His law had at last produced their inevitable results. The scourge of Babylon had in fact become the scourge of God. Here, as elsewhere in the Scriptures, is underscored a never-to-be-forgotten truth: "The way of the transgressor is hard *and* the wages of sin is death."

It is heartening, however, that out of the midst of dark tragedy and gloom there is always the bright light of hope. The weeping prophet himself looked above the misery of his present surroundings long enough to capture a glimpse of the wonderful grace of God. Lamentations 3:21-24 is a psalm of radiant beauty . . . a rose among thorns . . . a gem of the rarest quality . . . a true ray from the cross:

"This I recall to my mind, therefore have I hope. It is of the Lord's mercies that we are not consumed, because his compassions fail not. They are new every morning: great is thy faithfulness. The Lord is my portion, saith my soul; therefore will I hope in him."

The concluding chapter of Lamentations is a beautiful prayer for forgiveness and restoration of the Jewish nation. The author then put down his writing implements, rolled up his completed scroll, and rested with calm assurance that God was still in control of all things and that He would in His own time and own way, fulfill the promised destiny of His chosen race.

EZEKIEL

Author	Date of Writing	Theme	Key Personalities	Main Events
Ezekiel	592-570 B.C.	Judgment for Sin, Hope for Restoration	Ezekiel	Prophecies Concerning the Destruction of Jerusalem, Prophecies Concerning the Destruction of Other Nations, Prophecies Concerning Israel's Future Restoration

Ezekiel, whose name in Hebrew means "God strengthens," was, like Jeremiah, of priestly descent. He was the son of Buzi, of whom we know nothing except his name. Ezekiel apparently spent his early years in Jerusalem but was taken captive to Babylon in 597 B.C., along with King Jehoiachin and ten thousand other prominent citizens (2 Kings 24:14; Jeremiah 29:1, 2) during Nebuchadnezzar's second assault on Jerusalem. In Babylon, Ezekiel settled in his own house in a village near Nippur, along the river Chebar—Nebuchadnezzar's royal canal. He received his prophetic call at the age of thirty during the fifth year of his exile in Babylon. His prophecies spanned a period of some twenty-two years. Ezekiel was married (24:18), but his wife died of a stroke the same day the final siege of Jerusalem began (24:1, 15-18).

Ezekiel's entire prophetic ministry was to the exiles in Babylon. While Jeremiah continued to warn the inhabitants of Judah that Babylon would not only subjugate their land but would ultimately destroy it, Ezekiel was preaching the same message to the exiles in Babylon. This was not a very popular message (2:1, 4, 6), for many of the exiles held hope that their captivity would be short-lived. These hopes, however, were dashed and the prophecies of Jeremiah and Ezekiel confirmed when Nebuchadnezzar completed his infamous work and leveled Jerusalem to the ground eleven years after his second attack (586 B.C.).

The Book of Ezekiel consists of three divisions covering three principal subjects:

1. Prophecies concerning the fate of Jerusalem (1-24)
2. Prophecies against foreign nations (25-32)
3. Prophecies regarding Israel's future restoration (33-48)

The basic purpose of Ezekiel's message was to remind the exiles of the sins which had brought God's judgments on them—namely apostasy, foreign alliances, and idolatry—and to assure them of God's future blessing in keeping with His covenant. Ezekiel employed the use of symbols, proverbs, and parables to illustrate his message, making his style rather distinctive. He portrayed nations under the personification of animals, plants, and specific types of people. Jerusalem and Samaria are depicted as prostitutes (23:2, 3); the house of David as a lion's den (19:1), a vine (19:10, 17:6), or a cedar (17:3); Egypt as a cedar (31:3) or a crocodile (32:1); the Chaldeans (Babylonians) are pictured as an eagle; the city of Tyre is represented as a stately ship which will be sunk (27:5). Ezekiel himself engaged in symbolic acts which were obviously designed to illustrate certain truths. As a sign of famine, he lived on loathsome bread. He lay on one side for a long period of time to depict the discomfort of the siege. He shaved off his hair and beard and destroyed it to show the fate of Jerusalem. He dug through the wall and carried out an exile's baggage to depict the approaching captivity and exile. After each of the symbolic acts, the Lord spoke through Ezekiel and interpreted the meaning of each one (4:1-3; 4:4-8; 4:9-13; 5:1-12; 12:1-6, and so on). The phrase, "They [or ye] shall know that I am the Lord," is a dominant theme throughout the book and occurs over sixty times (6:7, 10, 13, 14, 7:4; 11:10; 12:15; 22:16; 33: 29; 38:23; and others).

Some of the more prominent passages in the Book of Ezekiel are the vision of the valley of dry bones—a preview of the restoration of the nation of Israel (37), the account of the original state of Satan (28), and the vision of a future city (48) much like the one described by John in

Revelation 21, 22. While John referred to the beautiful city he envisioned as the "new Jerusalem," Ezekiel simply stated that the glorious city shall be called, "The Lord is there" (Ezekiel 48:35).

DANIEL

Author	Date of Writing	Theme	Key Personalities	Main Events
Daniel	537 B.C.	God's Plan for the Ages	Daniel, Nebuchadnezzar, Shadrach, Meshach, Abednego, Belshazzar, Darius, Cyrus	Daniel's Deportation, Nebuchadnezzar's Dreams, The Fiery Furnace, Belshazzar's Feast, Defeat of Babylon by Darius, Daniel and the Lions' Den, Visions of Daniel

Daniel, whose name means "God is my judge," was carried captive as a teenager to Babylon in the first deportation by Nebuchadnezzar in 605 B.C. (1:1-7). This was eight years prior to Ezekiel's deportation and, like Ezekiel, Daniel's entire ministry was spent outside Palestine. A significant difference between the two prophets, however, was that Ezekiel ministered to the slave gangs of Babylon while Daniel prophesied to court officials and royalty.

Nothing is known of Daniel's parentage or family, but he apparently was of royal descent (1:3). Josephus, a noted Jewish historian, observed that Daniel and his three friends—Hananiah, Mishael, and Azariah (better known as Shadrach, Meshach, and Abednego)—were kin to King Zedekiah. Their nobility, youth, and exceptional mental acumen gained the attention of King Nebuchadnezzar. This resulted in their selection for training in the Chaldean language and special service in the Babylonian court. Although exiled in a strange land, these four young men remained loyal to their faith and uncompromising in their religious convictions. Their courage and moral stamina were evidenced by their refusal to eat the king's rations which they regarded as being ceremonially unclean (1:8-20).

Daniel's outstanding prophetic career spanned the entire seventy years of Jewish exile. During that time he not only witnessed the zenith of Babylon's power, but also its decline and overthrow by the Medo-Persians. During this period of political turbulence, military confrontation, and transfer of governmental power, it is most significant that Daniel was able to retain the favor of the succeeding heathen monarchs. He occupied a position of prominence under four kings of three different nations—Nebuchadnezzar and Belshazzar of Babylon, Darius the Mede, and Cyrus the Persian. Under Darius, he was appointed one of the three presidents of the land (6:1).

The first six chapters of Daniel are historical in character (although prophecy is not totally absent) and relate events in the life of Daniel. The last six chapters consist of a series of prophetic visions outlining "God's plan for the ages." These remarkable visions not only portray Israel's place in history, but they also trace the course of Gentile world power from Daniel's day to the second coming of Christ. Some of the more important prophecies of the Book of Daniel are listed below:

1. The future of Babylon, Persia, Greece, and Rome (Chapters 2, 7)
2. Prophecy of the Seventy Weeks (9:24-27)
3. Activities of the Antichrist (11:36-45)

Daniel also underscores several important Bible doctrines, such as personal separation (1:8; 3:12; 6:10; 9:2, 3; 10:2, 3), the doctrine of angels (8:16; 9:21; 10:13, 20, 21; 11:1), and the doctrine of the Resurrection (12:2). Favorite stories of the book include the following:

1. Shadrach, Meshach, and Abednego in the Fiery Furnace (chapter 3)
2. Daniel and the Handwriting on the Wall (chapter 5)
3. Daniel in the Lions' Den (chapter 6)

Daniel is unquestionably one of the most colorful personalities of the Bible. There is hardly a Sunday school student anywhere who has not been intrigued by the thrilling adventures of his life. The strength of his dedication, the courage of his conviction, the inspiration of his wisdom, and the purity of his life have all served to make his name a household word and to provide a lasting example of godly living.

Daniel lived to be an old man (in excess of ninety years) and died in the land of his forced adoption. However, before his death, he was permitted to see the return of his people to their homeland under the decree of Cyrus. Remembering the arrival of the first exiles in Babylon, the aged prophet no doubt wept as he watched the last of the caravans fade into the distance bound for Jerusalem. Although sad that he was too old and feeble to make the journey, he must have been filled with profound joy that he had lived to see the promise of God fulfilled. The captive was finally free. God had indeed kept His word.

HOSEA

Author	Date of Writing	Theme	Key Personalities	Main Events
Hosea	710 B.C.	God's Steadfast Love for Israel	Hosea, Gomer	Hosea's Marriage to Gomer, Birth of Their Three Children, Hosea's Messages to Israel

Hosea, whose prophetic office extended for sixty or more years, was a contemporary of Amos in Israel and of Isaiah and Micah in Judah. He prophesied to the Northern Kingdom of Israel, referring to it frequently as "Ephraim" after its largest tribe. Very little is known of Hosea's early life except that he was the son of Beeri. Although several references are made in his writings to the Southern Kingdom of Judah, he was, in all probability, a resident of Israel.

The name *Hosea* means "salvation" and is found in the Scriptures in various forms. It is the equivalent of Joshua— successor to Moses, to Hoshea—the last king of Israel, and, in its Greek form, to Jesus.

The period of Hosea's prophecy (782-715 B.C.) was one of abundance and material prosperity, but it was also one of political corruption and spiritual bankruptcy. Outwardly the nation appeared strong, but inwardly it was coming apart. Four of the seven kings of this period were murdered by those who succeeded them. Hosea's message of judgment at first seemed rather remote. However, by 732 B.C. Damascus had fallen to the Assyrians, and by 721 B.C. Samaria (Israel's capital city) had also fallen.

The Book of Hosea is the first and longest of the group we call the "minor prophets." It contains fourteen chapters which may be subdivided as follows:

1. Chapters 1-3—Hosea's Marital Difficulties and Their Implications for Israel

2. Chapters 4-14—Hosea's Messages to Israel

In the first section of the book, Hosea recounts his unhappy marital relationship with Gomer, who was either a prostitute at the time of their marriage or became one shortly thereafter. Her persistent sin of infidelity became a graphic example to the prophet of Israel's waywardness and spiritual adultery. The names of the three children born to their marriage were given to illustrate the impending fate of the nation. God instructed Hosea to call his first-born Jezreel, which means "sown or scattered by God." This no doubt referred to Israel's approaching exile. Loruhamah was the name given to the second child which meant "without compassion," indicating that when judgment fell, no mercy would be shown. The third child was called Loammi, meaning "not my people," signifying the climax of Israel's fate and her rejection and renunciation by God.

In spite of her unfaithfulness to him, Hosea's love for Gomer could not be quelled. His aching heart drove him to search for her in hopes of reconciling their broken marriage. He soon found her—despised and abandoned by her lovers and apparently sold as a slave. In love he purchased her freedom, tenderly forgave her, and restored her as his wife. Hosea's deep love for Gomer provided a beautiful example of God's steadfast love for unfaithful Israel. Although a time of discipline was necessary, God would not cast aside His love covenant with her forever.

Within His own perfect time plan, He, like Hosea, would find Israel in the slave market, pay the ransom price, and restore her to her rightful position as His own.

The latter section of the book (chapters 4-14) consists of a series of messages from Hosea to Israel. It contains appeals, denunciations, warnings, exhortations, and promises. What Jeremiah was to Judah, Hosea was to Israel—a broken-hearted prophet tenderly pleading for national repentance and a return to God. Unfortunately, the people did not listen. The message of the "prophet of love" went unheeded and judgment came.

JOEL

Author	Date of Writing	Theme	Key Personalities	Main Events
Joel	835 B.C.	The Day of the Lord		Locust Plague and Drought in Judah, Fasting and Prayer for Deliverance, Prophecy of Pentecost, The Day of the Lord

Joel is generally regarded to be among the earliest of the prophets, living near the time of Elijah and Elisha, approximately eight hundred years before Christ. He was, in all probability, a native of Jerusalem (1:9; 2:15-17, 23, 32; 3:1) and directed his entire ministry to the Southern Kingdom of Judah. Little information is given concerning Joel's background except that he was the son of Pethuel. His name means "Jehovah is God"—a very common name in the Old Testament, with no less than fourteen men identified by it.

The occasion of Joel's prophecy was a terrible plague of locusts which brought unbelievable devastation to the countryside. Crops, trees, and other forms of vegetation were stripped bare before the invading army of insects. In addition to this catastrophe, the nation was hit by severe drought followed by outbreaks of fire which further destroyed crops and pastureland. The combined effect of these multiple disasters was economic chaos, culminating in famine throughout the land. According to some authorities, these calamities may have lasted for as long as four years—bringing Judah to the very brink of collapse.

Joel viewed the nation's plight as a form of judgment for the sin and spiritual neglect of the people. He therefore issued a call for national repentance by means of a fast and "a solemn assembly," from which no one was to be exempted—not even babies or newlyweds (2:15-17).

The depth of Joel's concern was reflected in his instructions to the people:

"Rend your heart, and not your garments, and turn unto the Lord your God: for he is gracious and merciful, slow to anger, and of great kindness. . . . Let the priests, the ministers of the Lord, weep between the porch and the altar, and let them say, Spare thy people, O Lord, and give not thine heritage to reproach, that the heathen should rule over them" (2: 13, 17).

The central theme of the Book of Joel is his emphasis upon the "day of the Lord." This expression, appearing on at least five different occasions (1:15; 2:1, 2, 11, 31; 3: 14, 18), is used to denote God's intervention in the affairs of human history. Joel's use of the term not only applied to Judah's immediate crisis, but the keen eye of the prophet spanned the centuries and viewed the "day of the Lord" in connection with the startling events of the great tribulation period (2:1-11, 30, 31).

Joel is perhaps best known for his prophecy concerning the outpouring of the Holy Spirit. In this regard, he is sometimes referred to as the "prophet of Pentecost." It was Joel's inspired declaration that formed the basis for Peter's first Pentecostal sermon after he and 119 others had been filled with the Spirit:

"And it shall come to pass afterward, that I will pour out my spirit upon all flesh; and your sons and your daughters shall prophesy, your old men shall dream dreams, your young men shall see visions: And also upon the servants and upon the handmaids in those days will I pour out my spirit" (2:28, 29; see also Acts 2:16-18).

In response to Peter's powerful sermon, three thousand souls were saved, thus beginning a worldwide evangelistic crusade under the direction of the Holy Spirit—a crusade which will be continued in every generation until Jesus comes.

AMOS

Author	Date of Writing	Theme	Key Personalities	Main Events
Amos	755 B.C.	Justice and righteousness are marks of true religion.	Amos	Predictions of Judgment Against Various Nations, Amos's Three Sermons, Five Visions of Judgment, Restoration and Future Glory of Israel

Amos was an eighth-century prophet, an older contemporary of Hosea. His prophecies are dated during the reigns of Jeroboam II of Israel and Uzziah of Judah. This was a period of unprecedented material prosperity in the land. However, it was also one of gross idolatry, moral degeneracy, and social injustice—sins the prophet Amos felt compelled to expose in an effort to recall the nation from her backslidden condition.

Amos lived in the little town of Tekoa, about five miles southeast of Bethlehem. Although a resident of Judah, his mission was primarily to the Northern Kingdom of Israel. Amos identified himself as a layman called of God to be a prophet while engaged in humble occupation as a shepherd (1:1) and fruit picker (7:14). He described his unique calling: "I was no prophet, neither was I a prophet's son; but I was an herdman, and a gatherer of sycomore fruit: And the Lord took me as I followed the flock, and the Lord said unto me, Go, prophesy unto my people Israel" (7:14, 15).

The boldness of Amos in declaring the message of God is reminiscent of the manner of Elijah in the days of Ahab and Jezebel and of John the Baptist in the New Testament. He minced no words, made no pretenses, and proclaimed his message in unmistakable terms. He even dared to preach at Bethel, the very seat of the idolatrous calf worship in Israel. There he so angered Amaziah, the king's royal chaplain, that he was accused of treason (7:10, 11), of being a foreign intruder (7:12), and of trespassing on sacred property (7:13). He was finally expelled from the country, but only after he had fulfilled the purpose for which he came.

The name *Amos* means "load" or "burden." Probably no prophet in Jewish history ever displayed more zeal or dedication in the discharge of his calling than did Amos. The burden of the Lord was heavily upon him, and his restless spirit drove him to share the message God had given. The expression "thus saith the Lord" occurs some forty times throughout his writings.

The book itself consists of nine chapters, which may be subdivided into four divisions. Chapters 1 and 2 forecast judgment against Syria, Philistia, Tyre, Edom, Ammon, and Moab, as well as Judah and Israel. Chapters 3 through 6 contain three sermons of the prophet directed against Israel for her sins. Each of the sermons are easily identified beginning with the phrase, "Hear ye this word" (3:1; 4:1; 5:1). The third section of Amos's prophesy (chapters 7-9:8) consists of five visions of judgment involving locusts, fire, the plumbline, the basket of summer fruit, and the smiting of the altar. The remainder of chapter nine (verses 11-15) is the prophet's concluding remarks offering bright hopes of restoration and glory for the nation of Israel. Key verses of the book include 3:2, 3; 4:12; 5:24; 9:11.

OBADIAH

Author	Date of Writing	Theme	Key Personalities	Main Events
Obadiah	840 or 586 B.C.	The Destruction of Edom		Prophecy Regarding Edom

Obadiah is the shortest book of the Old Testament, consisting of only twenty-one verses. Nothing is known about the author except that his name means "servant of the Lord." At least twelve men in the Old Testament are identified by the name Obadiah, and any attempt to ascribe authorship to any one of them is at best conjecture.

The message of the book is concerned primarily with the destruction of Edom for aiding and abetting Judah's enemies during time of war. The prophet was very specific in assessing the war crimes for which Edom was to be judged:

1. She stood by while Jerusalem was invaded (verse 11).

2. She rejoiced over the captivity of the people (verse 12).

3. She actively participated in the sacking of Jerusalem (verse 13).

4. She set up roadblocks to prevent the escape of the Jewish people and turned over prisoners to the enemy (verse 14).

It is uncertain which invasion the Edomites participated in, since at least four major campaigns were launched against Judah during the period of the prophets:

1. By Shishak of Egypt, 926 B.C. (1 Kings 14:25, 26)

2. By the Philistines and the Arabians during the reigns of Jehoram, 848-841 B.C. (2 Chronicles 21:16, 17)

3. By King Joash of Israel, 790 B.C. (2 Kings 14: 13, 14)

4. By Babylon, 605-586 B.C. (2 Kings 24, 25)

This unfortunate lack of information also prevents accurate dating of the book. However, it is believed by many authorities that the attack by the Philistines and the Arabians is the one to which Obadiah referred.

The feud between Edom and Israel was an ancient one, dating back to the days of their progenitors, Jacob and Esau (Jacob being the father of Israel, Esau the father of Edom). The original conflict was over the birthright blessings which were rightfully Esau's, but were unscrupulously and deceptively obtained by Jacob (Genesis 25:27-34; 27: 1-46). The personal differences between the two brothers seem to have been resolved prior to their deaths. However, the animosity between their descendents continued to increase over the years (Numbers 20:14-20; 1 Samuel 14:47; 1 Kings 11:14-17; 1 Kings 11:14-25; 2 Chronicles 20:22; 2 Chronicles 21:8).

From the thirteenth to the sixth century B.C., the Edomites made their home in the rocky cliffs south of the Dead Sea, establishing Sela (Petra) as their capital. The rugged, mountainous terrain, with peaks jutting some two thousand feet in the air, provided natural defenses against the threat of hostile forces. Within their walled fortresses, the Edomites developed a false sense of security and felt that their cities were impregnable. With smugness they shouted to the world, "Who shall bring me down to the ground?" (verse 3). Through the prophet Obadiah, God responded to their arrogant attitude by saying, "Though thou exalt thyself as the eagle, and though thou set thy nest among the stars, thence will I bring thee down, saith the Lord" (verse 4).

The prophecy of Obadiah concerning the destruction of Edom was partially fulfilled in 312 B.C. when the Nabataeans, an Arab people, dislodged the Edomites from their cliff cities and drove them to Idumaea in Southern Palestine. Its fulfillment was completed in 70 A.D. when Titus (the Roman general) leveled Jerusalem, scattered the Jews, and completely wiped out the Edomites (Idumaeans). The Edomites, as incredible as it may seem, had finally laid aside their ancient feud long enough to join the Jews in their massive struggle to throw off the Roman yoke. In this final struggle, it is significant that the two brothers, Esau and Jacob (Israel and Edom), were at last united.

JONAH

Author	Date of Writing	Theme	Key Personalities	Main Events
Jonah	760 B.C.	1. Rebellion against God's will is a bitter and futile experience. 2. God's message is universal.	Jonah	Account of Jonah's Calling and Ministry to Nineveh

Jonah was an eighth-century prophet, a contemporary of Hosea and Amos. He was the son of Amittai and resided in Gath-hepher, a little town in lower Galilee about three miles from Nazareth. Jonah is best known for his preaching to the Ninevites. However, prior to the unusual events leading to that mission, Jonah was a prophet of some repute in the Northern Kingdom of Israel. Second Kings 14:25 indicates that Jonah's prophetic office was established during the reign of Jeroboam II (782-753 B.C.). Scripture also records that it was during this period that Israel regained her ancient boundaries from Hamath on the north to the Sea of Arabah on the south "according to the word of the Lord God of Israel, which he spake by the hand of his servant Jonah." Jonah's name in Hebrew means "dove." The Greek form of his name, *Jona* or *Jonas*, is used several times in the New Testament in reference to events of his life (Matthew 12:39-41; 16:4; Luke 11:29-32).

Jonah received a special call from God to pronounce judgment upon the great city of Nineveh because of its terrible wickedness. At that time, Nineveh was the capital of the powerful Assyrian empire and was located on the east bank of the Tigris River. Founded by Nimrod (Genesis 10:11) around 3,000 B.C., the city had grown to become one of the foremost cities of the then known world, with a population of over 120,000 (4:11). It was a city of splendor and grandeur, thirty miles long and ten miles wide, and boasted of beautiful gardens, refreshing waterways, and exquisite sculpture. Its massive walls were one hundred feet high and fifty feet wide—wide enough for four chariots to be driven abreast. There were fifteen entrances to the city, with lions and winged bulls guarding the gates. Nineveh was also the cultural center of its day, featuring a royal library containing ten thousand clay tablets with information on such subjects as law, science, literature, astronomy, history, chronology, commerce, and religion.

In spite of the apparent cultural development of the Assyrians, they were an idolatrous people (worshiping no less than thirteen different gods), grossly immoral, and barbaric. They were fierce and warlike, bent on world conquest. The merciless and cruel manner in which they treated their victims struck terror in the hearts of the surrounding nations.

It was this knowledge, perhaps, that caused Jonah to shrink from his assigned task at Nineveh, taking instead a ship bound for Tarshish (a seaport of southern Spain). He secretly hoped that by his absence, God would follow through with his plan to exterminate this heathen nation from the earth (4:2). Whatever his motives, his flagrant disobedience to God's will could not go unchecked. Subsequently, God arranged a series of miracles (six in all) to awaken Jonah's conscience and to insure that Nineveh was given opportunity to hear His message. The miracles as recorded in the Book of Jonah are as follows:

1. The Storm at Sea—"The Lord sent out a great wind" (1:4).

2. The Great Fish—"The Lord had prepared a great fish" (1:17).

3. Disgorging of Jonah by the Fish at the Command of God—"The Lord spake unto the fish, and it vomited out Jonah upon the dry land" (2:10).

4. The Gourd—"The Lord God prepared a gourd" (4:6).

5. The Worm—"God prepared a worm" (4:7).

6. The Scorching East Wind—"God prepared a vehement east wind" (4:8).

After Jonah had learned several difficult lessons in God's school of experience, he was given a second chance to preach at Nineveh—whereupon a city-wide revival occurred. From the king on his throne to the peasant in his hut, the people responded en masse to Jonah's message by calling a fast and repenting in sackcloth and ashes. Seeing their sincerity of heart, God heard their prayer, forgave their sin, and withheld His previously announced judgment.

Concerning the life and times of Jonah, it is noteworthy that Christ compared His resurrection to Jonah's three-day imprisonment in the fish (Matthew 12:40; 16:4) and contrasted His own rejection by the Jews to the openness and responsiveness of the Ninevites (Gentiles) to the preaching of Jonah (Matthew 12:41).

MICAH

Author	Date of Writing	Theme	Key Personalities	Main Events
Micah	700 B.C.	Justice, mercy, and humility are virtues of a true follower of God.	Micah	Judgment of Samaria and Judah, Judgment Upon the Leaders and False Prophets, The Future Kingdom of the Messiah

Micah, whose name means "who is like God," exercised his prophetic office during the reigns of Jotham, Ahaz, and Hezekiah (1:1). He was a native of the little rural village of Moresheth, located near the southwestern borders of Judah. Though a resident of the Southern Kingdom, Micah's prophecies were directed to both Israel and Judah. He was contemporary with Hosea, Amos, and Isaiah. And, like his contemporaries, he identified and denounced the prominent sins of his day—namely, idolatry, social injustice, and the hollow religious observances of both the people and their leaders.

Micah was a man of strong character and conviction, an uncompromising preacher of righteousness. His absolute confidence in his calling and mission as a prophet of God gave him boldness to speak to a nation who, for the most part, turned a deaf ear to his message. In reference to his ministry he declared:

"I am full of power by the spirit of the Lord, and of judgment, and of might, to declare unto Jacob his transgression, and to Israel his sin" (3:8).

Micah left no stones unturned in his attempts to bring about a genuine awakening throughout the land. He pronounced judgment upon Israel for her "incurable wound of idolatry" (see 1:5-16), rebuked the false prophets who "divined for money" (see 3:5-12), condemned the people for preferring to listen to false prophets under the influence of alcohol rather than one under the influence of the Holy Spirit (2:11), and exposed the dishonest merchants who cheated the people by means of "scant measures, wicked balances, and deceitful weights" (see 6:10-12).

Micah was deeply sensitive to the problems of the poor and the oppressed. He exposed and condemned the rich, powerful landowners who coveted and illegally confiscated the property of the poor (2:1-4; 3:1-4). Because of his relentless campaign against those who mistreated the less fortunate, Micah has come to be regarded as the "prophet of the poor" and the "champion of the people's cause." It might be said of him as was said of Jesus, "The common people heard him gladly."

The basic theme of Micah's message is found in chapter 6, verse 8, "He hath shewed thee, O man, what is good; and what doth the Lord require of thee, but to do justly, and to love mercy, and to walk humbly with thy God?" The book itself consists of three prophetic addresses, each of which are introduced by the word *hear* (1:2; 3:1; 6:1).

1. Chapters 1 and 2—Judgment upon Israel and Judah for their sins

2. Chapters 3 through 5—Judgment upon the leaders of the nation, the wicked princes, and the false prophets (chapter 3). The conclusion of this address (chapters 4 and 5) announces the coming kingdom of the Messiah.

3. Chapters 6 and 7—Call to repentance, with assurance of future blessings for Israel

The more significant prophecies found in the Book of Micah include: The Fall of Samaria in 721 B.C. (1:6, 7), The Invasion of Judah by Sennacherib (1:9-16), The Fall of Jerusalem and the Destruction of the Temple in 586 B.C. (3:12; 7:13), The Exile in Babylon (4:10), Israel's Return From Captivity and Her Future Glory (4:1-8, 13; 7:11, 14-17), and The Birthplace of the Messiah in Bethlehem (5:2). Favorite verses in the book include 6:8, 7:7, 7:18, 19.

NAHUM

Author	Date of Writing	Theme	Key Personalities	Main Events
Nahum	663-612 B.C.	God's judgment is sure and swift upon the wicked.	Nahum	Prophecy of Nineveh's Destruction

The subject of Nahum's prophecy is the destruction of Nineveh, the capital of the great Assyrian empire. A little more than a century before Nahum's time, Jonah preached in the streets of Nineveh and forecast God's judgment upon the city for its wickedness. In response to Jonah's preaching, the people—from the least to the greatest—repented in sackcloth and ashes, causing God to stay His hand of judgment. During the intervening years, however, the sound of Jonah's voice had long since faded. His message concerning the one God, Jehovah, had been cast aside with the rubble of history. Now, Assyria had arisen to the height of her power and had become the absolute master of the world. Her ruthless war machine had ground city after city and nation after nation into the dust. Every attempt at overthrow had failed, and the very mention of the Assyrian name caused people to tremble. Her kings boasted of the terrible atrocities which, among other things, consisted of boiling their victims in tar, impaling them on poles, skinning them alive, and ripping limbs from their bodies. Their cruelty, wickedness, and heathenish practices could no longer be tolerated by God. The mercy He so generously demonstrated a century earlier had now turned to wrath. Nahum the prophet was called upon to issue the nation's death warrant.

Nahum's prophecy is easily subdivided by chapters:

1. Chapter 1 is a psalm of triumph over the impending fall of Nineveh.

2. Chapter 2 describes the siege and destruction of Nineveh.

3. Chapter 3 sets forth the reasons for her downfall.

In the first chapter, Nahum gave a beautiful description of the character of God and graphically portrayed His attitude both toward the wicked and the righteous. Toward the wicked He is jealous of His honor (1:2), an avenger (1:2), full of wrath (1:2), unwilling to acquit the wicked (1:3), indignant (1:6), fierce in anger (1:6), and possesses great power (1:3-6). Toward those who love Him He is slow to anger (1:3), good (1:7), a stronghold in the day of trouble (1:7), recognizes their trust in Him (1:7), and delivers them from the enemy (1:15).

In chapter 2 Nahum described the battle of Nineveh with such clear and forcible language that one can almost hear the noise of the battle, see the flaming torches of the chariots as they jostle in the streets, and watch aghast as the black specter of death takes its awful toll.

Chapter 3 identifies the reasons for Nineveh's judgment. The list includes the sins of murder, lying, robbery, witchcraft, extortion, oppression, and pride. Such a catalog of sins was a clear verdict against the Assyrian nation. Nahum's prophecy was not a call to repentance, but the statement of a certain and final doom. So complete was to be her destruction that the name of Assyria would be forever blotted out.

Nahum's prophecy came to pass within a few years. It is quite possible that he lived to see its fulfillment. In 612 B.C., through an alliance of the Medes, Babylonians, and Scythians, the great city of Nineveh was conquered and destroyed. This was followed a short time later by the total collapse of the empire.

In accordance with Nahum's prophecy (2:6), a sudden rise of the Tigris River carried away part of the wall of the city, assisting the attacking armies in the overthrow. Also in accordance with Nahum's prophecy (3:13, 15), the city was

partially destroyed by fire. Nineveh was so completely oblit-
erated that it could never rise again. In fact, its location
was lost to history. Many Bible critics even denied that such
a city existed until its remains were discovered during the
1800's.

Unfortunately, very little is known about the background of
the prophet Nahum, except that he came from Elkosh (1:
1). The exact location of Elkosh has not been determined;
however, some authorities identify it with Capernaum, which
means, "city of Nahum." It is reasoned that the original
name of the city was Elkosh, but was later changed to
Capernaum in honor of its most distinguished citizen.
Nahum's name means "comfort" or "consolation." This probably refers to the consolation his prophecy offered to Judah
that "the wicked shall no more pass through thee; he is
utterly cut off" (1:15).

HABAKKUK

Author	Date of Writing	Theme	Key Personalities	Main Events
Habakkuk	607 B.C	The just shall live by faith.	Habakkuk	Habakkuk's Questions, God's Answers, Habakkuk's Psalm of Prayer and Praise

The prophet Habakkuk was a contemporary of Zephaniah and Jeremiah, all of whom predicted the Babylonian invasion and destruction of Jerusalem. Habakkuk prophesied shortly before Nebuchadnezzar first invaded Judah in 605, taking Daniel and others as captives to Babylon. The conditions in Judah at the time were extremely unstable, King Josiah having been slain in 609 B.C. by Pharaoh Necho on his march to Palestine to meet the Babylonians. Upon Josiah's death, the Jews had installed Jehoahaz (Josiah's son) as king. But he was deposed after three months by Necho, who installed Jehoahaz' brother, Eliakim (Jehoiakim), as king in his stead. Jehoiakim was a weak and wicked king whom the prophet Jeremiah rebuked, saying, "Thine eyes and thine heart are not but for thy covetousness, and for to shed innocent blood, and for oppression, and for violence, to do it" (Jeremiah 22:17).

Nothing is known of the background of the prophet Habakkuk except that his name in Hebrew means "embrace" —a fitting description of his devotion to God. In reviewing the Book of Habakkuk, four things are immediately noticeable about the prophet:

1. He was a man of problems.
2. He was a man of prayer.
3. He was a man of faith.
4. He was a man of song.

Habakkuk's problems revolved around two troubling questions. The first—Why did God allow wicked practices to continue in Judah? (1:2-4). God's reply to the prophet's question was that it would only be a matter of time until the

Babylonians would wield the sword of judgment against Judah (1:5-11). This answer further confused the prophet bringing to focus the second question—Why would God use wicked people to punish Judah? (1:12-2:1). God responded by assuring Habakkuk that Babylon would not go unpunished and that within his own time frame she would receive her just dues.

An admirable trait of the prophet Habakkuk was that he was a man of prayer. Overwhelmed by the violence, injustice, oppression, and wickedness of his day, he brought his burden to God in prayer. Thus, he demonstrated his confidence in the strength and power that God alone can supply in the time of desperate need.

The message of Habakkuk further demonstrated that he was a man of tremendous faith. In fact, the central theme of God's answer to Habakkuk during his period of questioning and confusion is recorded in Habakkuk 2:4—"the just shall live by his faith." This statement is quoted in at least three other books of the Bible—Romans 1:17, Galatians 3:11, and Hebrews 10:38. This was also the same great truth that Martin Luther discovered while searching the Scriptures, becoming the principle upon which the Protestant Reformation was founded.

Habakkuk was also a man of song. The third chapter of Habakkuk's prophecy is a magnificent psalm of praise to God. It is interesting to observe the progression of Habakkuk's experience from problems to prayer to faith to singing. This provides an excellent pattern for the Christian during the crisis experiences of life. Few passages in the Word of God exceed Habakkuk's song of exaltation and praise. It rises like a grand crescendo of music, extolling the majesty and greatness of God. It concludes with the triumphant words, "Yet I will rejoice in the Lord, I will joy in the God of my salvation. The Lord God is my strength, and He will make my feet like hinds' feet, and he will make me to walk upon mine high places" (3:18, 29).

ZEPHANIAH

Author	Date of Writing	Theme	Key Personalities	Main Events
Zephaniah	625 B.C.	The Day of the Lord	Zephaniah	Judgment Upon Judah, Judgment Upon Various Gentile Nations, Prophecies Regarding the Millennial Age

Zephaniah was a prophet of the Southern Kingdom of Judah, a contemporary of Nahum and Jeremiah. He apparently was of noble birth, the son of Cushi and the great, great-grandson of King Hezekiah, sometimes called Hizkiah (1:1). Zephaniah prophesied during the reign of King Josiah, which extended from 640-609 B.C. Josiah came to the throne at the young age of eight, following the assassination of his father, Amon, who served as king only two years. His grandfather, Manasseh, was one of the most wicked kings in Judah's history, openly endorsing the practice of idolatry and the rejection of the worship of Jehovah. Josiah's reign fell into two separate periods: the Pre-Reformation Period (640-621 B.C.) and the Reformation Period (621-609 B.C.). Josiah was regarded among the "good kings of Judah," and his great reformation begun in 621 B.C. was one of the most significant events during his reign. Among the reforms Josiah instituted was the repairing of the Temple with renewed emphasis upon true worship, destruction of the groves and shrines of Baal and Molech, execution of the idolatrous priests, and renewed emphasis upon the importance of God's Word (2 Kings 22, 23). Although a background figure, Zephaniah's preaching was undoubtedly a significant factor in bringing about these reforms throughout the land.

Zephaniah's prophecy consists of only three chapters, the theme of which is "the day of the Lord." This same expression used by Obadiah (verse 15), Joel (1:15), and Amos

94

(5:18-20) was identified by Zephaniah in relationship to the day of God's judgment. He forecast not only the judgment of Judah and Israel, but also the Gentile nations of Philistia, Moab, Ammon, Ethiopia, and Assyria. It is interesting to note that within a twenty-year period, all of these nations lay under the heel of the Babylonian empire—thus fulfilling the word of the prophet. Zephaniah described the "great day of the Lord" as a day of terrible calamity:

> "That day is a day of wrath, a day of trouble and distress, a day of wasteness and desolation, a day of darkness and gloominess, a day of clouds and thick darkness, A day of the trumpet and alarm against the fenced cities, and against the high towers. And I will bring distress upon men, that they shall walk like blind men, because they have sinned against the Lord: and their blood shall be poured out as dust, and their flesh as the dung" (1:15-17).

Zephaniah, as did all the prophets, not only predicted the judgment of the various nations, but set forth the reasons for their downfall. Among the reasons given for Judah's overthrow was their worship of Baal (introduced by the Phoenicians and Canaanites) and of Molech, the fire god of the Ammonites which sometimes included human sacrifice. Additional sins which Zephaniah cited were the practice of astrology (1:5), greediness (3:1), failure to listen to the prophets (3:2), apostasy (3:2), and false prophets and priests (3:4).

Thankfully, the prophet Zephaniah did not conclude his writings after the first two chapters. Had he done so, his message would have ended on an extremely depressing note. Chapter 3:9-20 provides a glorious view of the millennial age when the Messiah himself shall reign (3:15) and the joys and blessings of His kingdom shall be forever established. During that time, Israel is promised that her name will be praised among all the people of the earth. A favorite verse in Zephaniah is found in chapter 3, verse 17:

> "The Lord thy God in the midst of thee is mighty;

he will save, he will rejoice over thee with joy; he will rest in his love, he will joy over thee with singing."

The ultimate conclusion of the prophet seems to be that God not only is a God of judgment, He is a God of grace— grace that will bring about a millennial age of peace and prosperity. It is interesting that Zephaniah's name means "hidden by Jehovah," which is perhaps suggestive of the overshadowing grace of God.

HAGGAI

Author	Date of Writing	Theme	Key Personalities	Main Events
Haggai	520 B.C.	The Rebuilding of the Temple	Darius, Haggai, Zerubbabel, Joshua	Rebuilding of the Temple, Haggai's Call for Personal Dedication

Very little is known about the background of the prophet Haggai. In his book and in Ezra 5:1 and 6:14, he is simply referred to as "Haggai the prophet." He, along with the prophets Zechariah and Malachi, belong to the postexilic period of Jewish history. Consequently, their message is concerned with the reestablishment of the Jews' national life in their own land. In all probability, Haggai was among the first group of exiles, led by Zerubbabel, who returned to Jerusalem in 536 B.C. under the edict of King Cyrus. Based upon the prophet's statement in 3:2, it is believed that he had seen the glory of Solomon's Temple before it was destroyed by the Babylonian army in 586 B.C. This being true, it is quite possible that the prophet would have been a very old man (in excess of eighty years) at the time his prophecies were given. His name in Hebrew means "my feast."

Upon Zerubbabel's arrival in Jerusalem with the first contingency of exiles, an altar was erected for the daily sacrifices (Ezra 3:2) and worship resumed. The foundation of the Temple was laid in the second year of their return (Ezra 3:8-13). However, efforts to rebuild the Temple were soon blocked by the mixed-blooded Samaritans who convinced the new king of Persia (having ascended the throne after the death of Cyrus) that the Jews in Jerusalem were intent upon insurrection. Nothing further was done for fifteen years. It was at this juncture that the voice of the prophet Haggai was heard, reprimanding the people for their indifference to the construction of God's house.

Next to Obadiah, the prophecy of Haggai is the shortest in the Old Testament, consisting of only two chapters (thirty-eight verses). They were delivered during a four-month period between August and December, 520 B.C. The book contains four appeals, each of which are introduced by the phrase "the word of the Lord came." Haggai's prophecy may be subdivided as follows:

1. The Challenge to Rebuild the Temple (1:1-15)

2. The Challenge to Be Courageous in the Lord (2:1-9)

3. The Challenge to Cleanliness of Life (2:10-19)

4. The Challenge of the Future (2:20-23)

The first appeal was an exhortation to Zerubbabel and the high priest, Joshua, to undertake the immediate rebuilding of the Temple. In this section the prophet reproved the people for permitting their own selfish interest to exceed their concern for the rebuilding of the Temple. In the second address, the message was primarily one of encouragement to the builders to continue with the project until it was completed. The third message was a spiritual one in which the prophet urged the people to sanctify themselves, not merely by outward conformity to ritual, but through total obedience to the will and Word of God. The fourth exhortation was a brief prophetic glimpse of the time when Christ will rule the nations of the world.

ZECHARIAH

Author	Date of Writing	Theme	Key Personalities	Main Events
Zechariah	520-518 B.C.	Restoration of Israel and the Future Reign of the Messiah	Zechariah	Zechariah's Call to Repentance, Zechariah's Eight Visions, The Messianic Kingdom

Zechariah, whose name means "God remembers," was the son of Berechiah and the grandson of Iddo the priest. Ezra 5:1 and 6:14 identifies him as the son of Iddo, which probably means that Berechiah had died early, leaving Zechariah the immediate successor to his grandfather. Zechariah, like Jeremiah and Ezekiel before him, was both prophet and priest and probably began his ministry quite young (Zechariah 2:4). Zechariah most likely was born in Babylon and returned with the first caravan of exiles under Zerubbabel. He was contemporary with the prophet Haggai. Along with him, Zechariah encouraged the rebuilding of the Temple which had been destroyed in the Babylonian invasion (586 B.C.). There is a notable difference, however, between the prophecies of Zechariah and those of Haggai. Although both were instrumental in motivating the leaders of the Jewish community to reconstruct the Temple, Zechariah's prophecies are concerned to a greater degree with spiritual change.

The Book of Zechariah is one of consolation and hope, beginning with a call to repentance and concluding with significant prophecies concerning the return and reign of Christ. With the exception of Isaiah, Zechariah predicted more about the coming Messiah than did any other prophet. Prophecies concerning the first coming of Christ include 3:8; 9:9, 16; 11:11-13; 12:10; 13:1, 6. Prophecies regarding His second coming include 6:12 and 14:1-21.

Zechariah's prophecy may be subdivided as follows:
1. Introduction and Call to Repentance (1:1-6)
2. Zechariah's Eight Visions (1:7-6:15)
3. The Prophet's Address in the Fourth Year of Darius
   (7, 8)
4. Prophecy Regarding Gentile World Powers and the
   Future Messianic Kingdom (9-14)

Inasmuch as Zechariah was a postexilic prophet, there
appears to have been a threefold purpose for his writings:
(1) to bolster Israel's confidence in the full and complete
restoration of Zion, (2) to assure Israel of the judgment and
overthrow of her enemies, and (3) to announce the universal
reign of the Messiah.

The real beauty of the Book of Zechariah lies in the glori-
ou' hope he offered to Israel concerning her future Messiah.
The vividness and clarity of the prophet's description reads
like an advanced biography of the life of Christ. He is
portrayed as the branch (3:8), God's servant (3:8), the shepherd (9:16; 11:11), and the smitten shepherd (13:7). Major
prophecies concerning the life of Christ include (1) His triumphal entry into Jerusalem on a colt (9:9), (2) His be-
trayal for thirty pieces of silver (11:12, 13), (3) the piercing of His hands and feet (12:10), (4) His return to the
Mount of Olives (14:3-8), (5) His power to remove iniquity
(chapter 3), (6) His rejection by Israel (chapter 11), and
(7) the destruction of Israel's enemies, salvation of Jerusalem, and the millennial reign of the Messiah over all the
world (chapter 14).

Zechariah also provides us with a prophetic glimpse of the
suffering Savior on Calvary, declaring, "In that day there
shall be a fountain opened to the house of David . . . for
sin and for uncleanness" (13:1). "And I will pour upon the
house of David, and upon the inhabitants of Jerusalem, the
spirit of grace and of supplications: and they shall look
upon me whom they have pierced" (12:10).

MALACHI

Author	Date of Writing	Theme	Key Personalities	Main Events
Malachi	450-400 B.C.	Obedience results in God's favors and blessing.	Malachi	God's Love for Israel, God's Complaints Against Israel, God's Forthcoming Judgment

Malachi, whose name means "my angel" or "my messenger," is the last of the Old Testament prophets. His prophecies conclude a 1,000-year period of prophetic utterances (Moses through Malachi) by a noble breed of men who were called and anointed to declare God's message to Israel. The closing book of the Old Testament canon, the Book of Malachi is sometimes referred to as "the seal" of the prophets. After Malachi, the voice of a prophet was not heard in Israel for some four hundred years.

Malachi's personal history is not known. However, he probably was a contemporary of Nehemiah (compare 2:8 with Nehemiah 13:15; 2:10-16 with Nehemiah 13:23; 3:7-12 with Nehemiah 13:10). He prophesied approximately one hundred years after the Jews returned from captivity to their homeland. By this time, the city of Jerusalem and the "second temple" (Zerubbabel's Temple) had been built, but the early enthusiasm of the people had subsided. Following a period of revival under Nehemiah (Nehemiah 10:28-39), the people and the priests had backslidden and had lapsed into mechanical observances of the law. Recognizing the developing state of apostasy, the prophet Malachi issued a call to repentance and a firm warning to the disobedient and rebellious.

The prophecy of Malachi consists of three chapters and may be subdivided as follows:

Chapter 1—God's Love for Israel

Chapter 2—God's Complaints Against Israel

Chapter 3—God's Judgment of the People

Malachi expressed God's love for Israel in the first chapter. But at the same time, he reminded the people that they had failed to respond with true devotion to God (1:1-5). In chapter 2, Malachi blamed the spiritual condition of the nation primarily upon the priests who had polluted God's altar and offered unworthy sacrifices (1:6-2:4). The priests were further accused of failing to give proper instruction in God's law, thereby causing many to stumble (2:5-9). Malachi also condemned the men for divorcing their wives and marrying women of idolatrous nations (2:10-17), a practice prohibited by the law of Moses (Exodus 34:14-16 and Deuteronomy 7:3). Violation of this law had been a major factor in introducing idolatry into Israel, and Malachi saw this practice as a renewed threat to the true worship of Jehovah. Malachi is also noted for his strong emphasis upon the Lord's tithe:

"Will a man rob God? Yet ye have robbed me. But ye say, Wherein have we robbed thee? In tithes and offerings. Ye are cursed with a curse: for ye have robbed me, even this whole nation. Bring ye all the tithes into the storehouse, that there may be meat in mine house, and prove me now herewith, saith the Lord of hosts, if I will not open you the windows of heaven, and pour you out a blessing, that there shall not be room enough to receive it" (3:8-10).

The third chapter of Malachi deals with God's judgment which the prophet saw in relationship to the end-time events. He placed considerable emphasis on "the day of the Lord," which he referred to at least six times throughout his prophecy (1:11, implied; 3:2, 17; 4:1, 3, 5). Thus, the Old Testament closes with a final promise of the advent of the Messiah and the day of the Lord.

Malachi's style is quite unique among the prophets and consists of a question and answer approach. He asks at least twenty-three questions throughout his book, followed by answers to those questions. The expression "saith the Lord of hosts" occurs twenty times in Malachi's short prophecy of fifty-five verses.

REVIEW — UNIT 4

(Isaiah—Malachi)

1. List the major prophets.
2. List the minor prophets.
3. Discuss briefly the background and personal history of each of the prophets.
4. The key word in the Book of Isaiah is _____.
5. At the time of Jeremiah's prophecies, three major powers were vying for world supremacy: _____, _____, and _____.
6. Multiple choice. Ezekiel is regarded as a prophet of the (a) preexilic period, (b) Exile period, (c) postexilic period.
7. _____'s outstanding prophetic career spanned the entire seventy years of Jewish exile.
8. Samaria was destroyed by the _____ in 722 B.C.
9. Jerusalem was destroyed by the _____ in 586 B.C.
10. The name of Hosea's wife was _____.
11. _____ is noted as the "prophet of Pentecost."
12. List three of Amos's five visions of judgment.
13. Obadiah's prophecy concerned the nation of _____.
14. Jonah's prophecy was directed primarily to the city of _____.
15. What prophet is known as "the prophet of the poor"?
16. Nahum's name means _____ or _____.
17. What prophet is identified as a man of problems, a man of prayer, a man of faith, and a man of song?
18. The theme of Zephaniah's prophecy is _____.
19. Name the three postexilic prophets.
20. Name the prophet who foretold of Christ's triumphal entry into Jerusalem.

UNIT 5

MATTHEW

Author	Date of Writing	Theme	Key Personalities	Main Events
Matthew	A.D. 60's	Christ—The King	Jesus, John the Baptist, The Apostles	Life of Jesus

The New Testament consists of twenty-seven books written by at least eight different authors over a period of about fifty years. These books may be subdivided as follows:

The Gospels	Early Church History	Pauline Epistles	
Matthew	The Acts of	Romans	1 Thessalonians
Mark	the Apostles	1 Corinthians	2 Thessalonians
Luke		2 Corinthians	1 Timothy
John		Galatians	2 Timothy
		Ephesians	Titus
		Philippians	Philemon
		Colossians	Hebrews (?)

General Epistles		Prophecy
James	2 John	Revelation
1 Peter	3 John	
2 Peter	Jude	
1 John		

The term *New Testament*, applied to the second half of the Bible, literally means "new covenant" and marks a distinct change in God's method of dealing with fallen man.

The "old covenant" (Old Testament) was given through Moses at Mount Sinai and emphasized holiness by law. The "new covenant" (New Testament) came through the gift of God's Son and emphasized holiness by the grace of Calvary (Luke 22:20; Matthew 26:28; 1 Corinthians 11:25). Thus, the entire message of the New Testament centers around the person of Jesus Christ—His birth, life, ministry, death, burial, resurrection, ascension, and Second Coming.

Matthew appears first in the order of New Testament books and is also the first of the four Gospels. Although each of the evangelists (Matthew, Mark, Luke, and John) writes from a different perspective and for different audiences, the four Gospels blend together beautifully to form one grand portrait of the world's long-awaited Redeemer.

Matthew, who was surnamed Levi (Mark 2:14), was a tax collector (publican) who worked for the Roman government (Matthew 9:9). As such, he was despised by his fellow countrymen and regarded as a traitor to the Jewish cause. Nevertheless, he was selected by Christ to be numbered among the twelve apostles (Matthew 10:3; Acts 1:13). Upon the call of Christ, he promptly left the "receipt of custom" and became a devout follower of the Lord. Soon after his conversion, Matthew gave a "great feast" (Luke 5:29) to introduce his friends to Christ. This event was attended by a large number of "publicans and sinners." The fact that Christ dared to associate with such undesirables drew sharp criticism from the scribes and Pharisees, whereupon the Lord issued His famous declaration—"I came not to call the righteous, but sinners to repentance" (Luke 5:32). Very little is known of Matthew's life and ministry, but it is believed that he preached in Palestine for several years after the resurrection of Jesus and then became a missionary to foreign lands. He is best known throughout the Christian world for the Gospel that bears his name.

The Gospel of Matthew was written from a Jewish point of view and designed primarily to prove that Jesus of Nazareth was the Messiah of Old Testament prophecy. The book forms a strong link between the Old and New Testaments, containing no less than fifty-three direct quotations from the Old Testament, plus seventy-six allusions to it. With remarkable force and skill, Matthew traced the major events in the life of Christ and interpreted them as fulfilling the word of the prophets. Thirteen times he used the expression "that it might be fulfilled which was spoken of the Lord by the prophet" (1:22, 23; 2:5, 15, 17, 23; 3:3, 15; 4:14).

Nine times Matthew referred to Jesus as the Son of David, thus showing His royal descent and His rightful position as the promised Ruler of Israel. From the inquiry of the wise men—"Where is he that is born King of the Jews" (2:2), to the inscription over the Cross—"THIS IS JESUS THE KING OF THE JEWS" (27:37)—every chapter reflects the glory and majesty of King Jesus. The word *king* appears twenty times throughout the book and the word *kingdom* some fifty-five times. The expression "kingdom of heaven" is found on at least thirty-three different occasions and "kingdom of God" four times.

Matthew also gave particular attention to the teachings of Jesus and portrayed Him as the "great teacher of Israel." Of special importance are the Sermon on the Mount (chapters 5-7) which includes the Beatitudes (5:3-12), the Lord's Prayer (6:9-13), the Kingdom Parables (chapter 13), and the Olivet Discourse Concerning Future Events (chapters 24, 25).

MARK

Author	Date of Writing	Theme	Key Personalities	Main Events
Mark	A.D. 50's	Christ—The Servant	Jesus, John the Baptist, Apostles, Others	Life of Jesus

Although not specifically identified in the book as its author, John, whose surname was Mark, is generally credited with the authorship of the second Gospel (Acts 12:12, 25). John was his Jewish name; Mark (Marcus) was adopted from the Romans and became a part of his identity. John Mark was a cousin of Barnabas (Colossians 4:10) and the son of Mary, a woman of considerable wealth and position who resided in Jerusalem. She was an early convert to the Christian faith and opened her house for prayer meetings and other Christian gatherings (Acts 12:12). It was such a meeting to which Simon Peter reported after his miraculous deliverance from prison by the angel (Acts 12:1-17). It is quite possible that John Mark was a convert of Simon Peter, although this is uncertain. However, it is evident from the Scriptures that a strong bond of friendship developed between Peter and the young man Mark. Writing in later years, Peter referred to him as "Marcus my son" (1 Peter 5:13). It is generally agreed that Mark received much of the information in his Gospel from Peter and consequently became known as "the interpreter" of Peter.

Mark also had the unique privilege of accompanying Paul and Barnabas on their first missionary journey. But for unexplained reasons, John Mark left the missionaries at Perga and returned to Jerusalem. This act was not appreciated by Paul; subsequently, when Barnabas wanted to take John Mark along on the second missionary journey, Paul refused. The issue became so acute between Paul and Barnabas that they agreed to part ways. Paul took Silas and Barnabas remained loyal to his cousin John Mark, thus forming two missionary teams. Paul's view of Mark was later modified. In writing to Timothy during his imprisonment at Rome, he directed Timothy to bring Mark with him, stating: "He is profitable to me for the ministry" (2 Timothy 4:11).

Mark's Gospel is the shortest of the four Gospels (sixteen chapters) and is generally considered to be the oldest written account of the life of Jesus. Unlike Matthew, Mark's Gospel was not written for a Jewish audience but rather for Gentiles. It was probably written from Rome and therefore omitted many of the things essential to Jewish thought, such as quotations from the prophets and the genealogy of Jesus. Mark is a book of action; while Matthew emphasizes discourses, the Book of Mark emphasizes deeds. The key words in Mark's Gospel are *forthwith, straightway*, and *immediately*. These words appear no less than forty times throughout the book.

The theme of Mark's Gospel is found in 10:44, 45—"Whosoever of you will be the chiefest, shall be servant of all. For even the Son of man came not to be ministered unto, but to minister, and to give his life a ransom for many." Mark portrayed Christ as the tireless servant of God pouring out Himself for mankind. The author did not attempt to prove the deity of Christ but rather to allow His works to testify to His divinity. More than nineteen miracles are recorded in this short book, each of which demonstrates the supernatural power of the Master. Eight miracles are given to prove Christ's power over disease (1:31, 41; 2:3-12; 3: 1-5; 5:25; 7:32; 8:23; 10:46); five demonstrate His power over nature (4:39; 6:41, 49; 8:8, 9; 11:13, 14); four demonstrate His authority over demons (1:25; 5:1-13; 7:25-30; 9: 26); two reveal His conquest over death (5:42; 16:9).

The Gospel of Mark may be outlined as follows:
1. The Servant's Preparation (1:1-13)
2. The Servant's Work (1:14-10:52)
3. The Servant's Sacrifice (11:1-15:47)
4. The Servant's Honor (16:1-20)

LUKE

Author	Date of Writing	Theme	Key Personalities	Main Events
Luke	A.D. 60	Christ—The Son of Man	Mary, Joseph, Elizabeth, Zacharias, Anna, Simeon, the Apostles, Zacchaeus, Pilate, Herod, Others	Life of Jesus

Authorship for the third Gospel is attributed to Luke, "the beloved physician" (Colossians 4:14), who was a close friend and companion of the Apostle Paul. The name *Luke* occurs three times in the New Testament (Colossians 4:14; 2 Timothy 4:11; Philemon 24), and probably in all three, the third evangelist is the person spoken of. Some authorities believe that Luke was born in Antioch of Syria, while others believe that he was a native of Philippi in Macedonia (Acts 16:11-17, 40—20:5). In any event, it is quite certain that Luke was not born a Jew, for he is not listed among those "of the circumcision" by the Apostle Paul (compare Colossians 4:11 with verse 14). Luke accompanied Paul on at least part of his second missionary journey, joining him at Troas and traveling as far as Philippi, where he remained for a number of years. He also joined Paul on his third missionary journey and seems to have stayed with the apostle until after his execution in Rome. During his final imprisonment and shortly before his death, Paul wrote that Luke was with him (2 Timothy 4:11).

As a physician, Luke was a learned man. He no doubt received the finest education available in his day. His Gospel is by far the most beautiful and scholarly account of the life of Christ. Although he never saw Jesus personally, Luke was acquainted with many eye witnesses of the Lord's work from whom he gathered extensive and accurate information. His skillful pen, under the guidance of the Holy Spirit, thus produced one of the most inspiring books of the New Testament. In addition to his Gospel, Luke is also credited with the authorship of the Acts of the Apostles. Both books are written especially for the Gentiles and are addressed to an unknown person by the name of Theophilus.

The theme of Luke's Gospel is "Christ—The Son of Man." The expression "Son of man" is used no less than twenty-three times in Luke's Gospel and is used in reference to the humanity of our Lord. A basic purpose of Luke's writing is to portray a Savior who fully identifies Himself with every aspect of human life. As a man, He "wept over" the city (19:41); He "prayed more earnestly: and his sweat was as it were great drops of blood falling down to the ground" (22:44); He cried, "Father, into thy hands I commend my spirit" (23:46). He had a meal with Simon (7:36-50), with Martha and Mary (10:38-42), with a ruler of the Pharisees (14:1-24); He went home to visit with Zacchaeus (19:1-10); He ate a piece of broiled fish after His resurrection (24:41-43).

Among the more distinctive features of Luke's Gospel is the emphasis upon prayer. Christ is represented as a man of prayer on at least eleven occasions. The book also has three parables on prayer not found in the other Gospels—the friend at midnight (11:5-8), the unjust judge (18:1-8), and the Pharisee and the publican (18:9-14).

Luke's Gospel is also a book of singing, for he recorded no less than four great songs: The Magnificat—Mary's Song of Rejoicing (1:46-55), The Song of Zacharias (1:68-79), The Song of the Angels at the Birth of Jesus (2:8-14), and The Song of Simeon (2:29-32).

Another significant feature of Luke's Gospel is his emphasis upon womanhood. A number of women are mentioned, including Elizabeth, Mary, Anna, the Widow of Nain, the widow who appealed to the unrighteous judge, Martha and Mary, and others.

Luke recorded more of the Lord's parables than either

of the other three Gospel writers. He recorded a total of forty-five parables and illustrations. He alone recorded the stories of the rich man Lazarus, the rich fool, the Pharisee and publican, the Good Samaritan, and the prodigal son. Nineteen parables in Luke are not mentioned by any other writer.

Because of its beauty, accuracy, and intellectual brilliance, Luke's Gospel takes rank among the most loved books of the Bible. One of the most impressive verses of the Bible concerning the ministry of Jesus is found in Luke 19:10—"For the Son of man is come to seek and to save that which was lost."

JOHN

Author	Date of Writing	Theme	Key Personalities	Main Events
The Apostle John	A.D.85-90	Christ—The Son of God	Jesus, John the Baptist, The Apostles, Nicodemus, Martha, Mary, Lazarus, Pilate, Others	Life of Jesus

Authorship for the fourth Gospel is ascribed to the Apostle John. Although the date of writing is uncertain, it is believed to have been penned near the close of the first century (A.D. 85-90). It was probably written from the city of Ephesus where the Apostle John resided in the later years of his life.

John was the son of Zebedee and Salome (Matthew 4:21, Matthew 27:56, Mark 15:40) and the younger brother of James, who also became an apostle of Christ and suffered martyrdom under Herod Agrippa I (Acts 12:1, 2). The family operated a prosperous fishing business on the Sea of Galilee, which is confirmed by the fact that they had their own boat and employed servants to assist with the business (Mark 1:16-20).

John seems to have been one of the first two persons (the other being Andrew) to follow the Lord after He began His public ministry (John 1:35-40). Along with his older brother, John had been a disciple of John the Baptist prior to his introduction to Jesus (John 1:35-40). After hearing John the Baptist announce Christ to be "the Lamb of God, which taketh away the sin of the world" (John 1:29), he became an ardent follower of the Lord. John was a man of rare qualities and leadership ability, subsequently becoming one of the three "inner circle disciples." He was one of the three apostles whom Jesus chose to be with Him at the raising of Jairus' daughter (Mark 5:37; Luke 8:51), at the Transfiguration (Matthew 17:1; Mark 9:2; Luke 9:28), and at the agony in the garden (Matthew 26:37; Mark 14:33). At the Last Supper, John occupied the place next to Jesus at the table (John 13:23). He also followed Jesus from Gethsemane into the palace of the high priest and to the place of crucifixion. While on the Cross, Jesus commended His mother, Mary, to John's loving care, a responsibility he accepted without reservation (John 18:15; 19:27). Five times John is spoken of as the disciple "whom Jesus loved" (John 13:23; 19:26; 20:2; 21:7, 20).

An interesting sidelight into the personality of John is the nickname which Jesus gave to him and his brother James—*Boanerges*, which means "sons of thunder" (Mark 3:17). This name apparently had reference to their zeal, intensity, and quickness of temper (Luke 4:49; 9:52-56; Matthew 20:20-24).

After Pentecost, John was a companion of Peter on several occasions (Acts 3:1; 4:19; 8:14). He was in Jerusalem when Paul visited the city after his first missionary journey (Acts 15:6; Galatians 2:9). His ministry was a long and fruitful one; he was, without doubt, the last surviving apostle. In addition to his Gospel, John is credited with four other New Testament books—1, 2, and 3 John and the Revelation which he penned during his exile on the Isle of Patmos.

John's Gospel is one of the most remarkable testimonies to the deity of Christ in the entire New Testament. In support of Christ's deity, John recorded seven witnesses, seven miracles, and seven "I am's." The seven witnesses who attest to the deity of Christ are as follows: John the Baptist (1:34), Nathaniel (1:49), Simon Peter (6:69), Martha (11:27), Thomas (20:28), John the Apostle (20:31), and Christ himself (10:36). The seven miracles (or signs) are as follows: the turning of water into wine (2:1-11), the cure of the nobleman's son (4:46-54), the cure of the paralytic (5:1-18), the feeding of the multitude (6:6-13), the walking on the water (6:16-21), the

113

giving of sight to the blind (9:1-7), and the raising of Lazarus (11:1-45). The seven "I am's" are as follows: "I am the bread of life" (6:35); "I am the light of the world" (8:12); "Before Abraham was, I am" (8:58); "I am the good shepherd" (10:11); "I am the resurrection, and the life" (11:25); "I am the way, the truth, and the life" (14:6); and "I am the true vine" (15:1).

It is obvious that John wrote his Gospel as a supplement to the other three Gospels. Being the last written, John was able to identify rich and important facts the other writers had omitted, such as Christ's conversation with Nicodemus, His meeting with the Samaritan woman, and the marriage in Cana of Galilee. Through John alone we know about His discourse on the Comforter (the Holy Ghost), the mansions in His Father's house, and His beautiful prayer for His disciples. At most John only included about twenty days of our Lord's ministry in his Gospel. But the beauty and richness with which he described the events provide an unforgettable experience for those who share his devotion for God's Son.

Matthew revealed Christ to the Jews, Mark revealed Him to the Romans, Luke to the Greeks, but John wrote for all men everywhere. His Gospel is called a "universal Gospel." If, for some reason, we should suddenly be stripped of all the Bible with the exception of the Gospel of John, it would be complete enough and powerful enough to bring salvation to the entire world. It is a book of infinite value, infinite beauty, and infinite blessing.

REVIEW — UNIT 5

(Matthew—John)

1. How many books are there in the New Testament?
2. Name the books referred to as the Gospels.
3. The New Testament was written by _____ different authors over a period of about _____ years.
4. *New Testament* literally means _____.
5. _____ was the man who gave a great feast to introduce his friends to Christ.
6. The theme of Matthew's Gospel is _____.
7. Who is called "the interpreter of Peter"?
8. More than _____ miracles are recorded in Mark's Gospel.
9. Three key words in Mark's Gospel are _____, _____, and _____.
10. The theme of Mark's Gospel is _____.
11. Luke is called "_____."
12. The theme of Luke's Gospel is _____.
13. Luke recorded more of the Lord's _____ than either of the other three Gospel writers.
14. List the five books written by the Apostle John.
15. The Gospel of John was most likely written from the city of _____.
16. John's father's name was _____; his mother's name was _____; his brother's name was _____.
17. Five times John is spoken of as the disciple _____.
18. The nickname Christ gave to James and John *(Boanerges)* meant _____.
19. In support of Christ's deity, John recorded seven _____, seven _____, and seven _____.
20. _____'s Gospel is called a "universal Gospel."

115

UNIT 6

ACTS

Author	Date of Writing	Theme	Key Personalities	Main Events
Luke	A.D. 61	Witness	Peter, John, Paul	Outpouring of Holy Spirit, Growth of the Early Church, Conversion of Saul (Paul), Paul's Three Missionary Journeys

The fifth book of the New Testament is called "The Acts of the Apostles." However, from a historical perspective, it is primarily the Acts of Peter (chapters 1-12) and of Paul (13-20). While other figures appear throughout the book (Stephen, Philip, Barnabas, and James), Peter and Paul are by far the prevailing personalities. Since Acts does not provide a complete narrative of the work and ministry of all the apostles, other titles to the book have been suggested as being more appropriate—"Gospel of the Holy Spirit," "Acts of the Ascended Christ," "Acts of Apostolic Men."

Basically, the Book of Acts is the record of the spread of Christianity from the coming of the Holy Spirit on the Day of Pentecost to Paul's arrival in Rome some thirty years later. This was an important time in the history of the Christian movement, for it was during this period that the Church grew from infancy to extend itself to all parts of the "then known world." Several important events are recorded in the Book of Acts—the origin, nature, founding, and growth of the Church; the first conversions; the first opposition; the first discipline; the first persecution; the first organization; the first martyr; and the sending out of the first missionaries.

The key word in the Book of Acts is *witness*, mentioned over thirty times throughout the book. The key verse is Acts 1:8—"But ye shall receive power, after that the Holy Ghost is come upon you: and ye shall be witnesses unto me both in Jerusalem, and in all Judaea, and in Samaria, and unto the uttermost part of the earth." The concise, crystal clear tones of the Great Commission (Matthew 28:19, 20; Mark 16:15; Luke 24:46-48; Acts 1:8) were designed by the Lord to provide His followers with a definite sense of mission and purpose in the world and to chart an unmistakable course of action for His Church. The responsibility to share the message of Jesus with the whole world was never to be understood as an option of the Church, but rather as an obligation requiring its most devoted attention. Thus, the Book of Acts is a book of action, for it is the record of the great exploits of men anointed by the Holy Ghost. With the words of the Great Commission ringing loudly in their ears and a burning passion in their hearts, they hurried to tell the story. The name of Jesus was heard everywhere—in the streets, in the Temple, and from house to house. Wherever there was a man, there was a message. By the end of the Apostolic Age (approximately 100 A.D.), the Church under the direction of the Holy Spirit had reached as many as 500 thousand converts.

The miraculous spread of the Christian faith can be directly attributed to the outpouring of the Holy Ghost on the Day of Pentecost (Acts 2) and to the boldness with which the early church declared the message of Jesus. The term *Holy Spirit* (or Holy Ghost) is mentioned no less than seventy times throughout the Book of Acts.

Of special significance is the conversion of Saul of Tarsus (later called Paul) to Christ and his subsequent missionary activity (chapter 9). Selected as a "chosen vessel," Paul was destined to become an apostle, minister, missionary, author, and church leader *par excellence*. Few men have made the impact upon Christendom as did the great man Paul.

The Book of Acts also offers support to many of the major

117

doctrines of the Scriptures, including repentance (2:38; 3:19), water baptism (2:38; 8:37-39), baptism of the Holy Spirit (2:4; 10:46; 19:6), prayer (3:1; 4:31; 6:4), healing (3:1-11; 9:32-35), faith (16:25-31), and the Resurrection (26:8).

Like the third Gospel, authorship for the Book of Acts is ascribed to the beloved physician Luke. It is also dedicated to the person of Theophilus. Although nothing is known concerning the person of Theophilus, he was in all probability a Greek nobleman or Roman official who was interested in Christianity. His name means "friend of God."

REVIEW — UNIT 6

(Acts)

1. Although the fifth book of the New Testament is called "The Acts of the Apostles," it is primarily the Acts of _____ and _____.

2. Basically, the Book of Acts is the record of the spread of _____ from the coming of the _____ _____ on the Day of Pentecost to Paul's arrival in Rome some _____ years later.

3. Name three first-time events recorded in the Book of Acts.

4. The key word in Acts is _____.

5. Quote Acts 1:8.

6. By the end of the _____ Age, approximately 100 A.D., the Church under the direction of the Holy Spirit had reached as many as _____ converts.

7. Give two factors which contributed to the miraculous spread of Christianity.

8. The term _____ _____ is mentioned no less than seventy times throughout the Book of Acts.

9. The Book of Acts records the conversion of _____ to Christ and his subsequent missionary activities.

10. Name three major doctrines mentioned in the Book of Acts.

11. The author of Acts is _____.

12. Acts is addressed to _____.

UNIT 7

ROMANS

Author	Date of Writing	Theme	Key Personalities	Main Events
Paul	A.D. 58	Justification by Faith	Paul, Phoebe, Twenty-six people, identified in Paul's greetings to the Roman Church (chapter 16)	Development of Great Doctrinal Themes—Salvation, Justification

The writings of the Apostle Paul are referred to as the Pauline Epistles or letters. Thirteen in number, they appear in the King James Version, beginning with the Epistle to the Romans and concluding with Philemon. Some authorities also accept Paul as the author of Hebrews; if correct, this would bring the number of books ascribed to his credit to fourteen—approximately one half of the entire New Testament.

During his early years, Paul (whose Jewish name was Saul) was a resident of Tarsus, a city in Cilicia (Acts 22:39). Of his parents we know nothing, except that his father was of the tribe of Benjamin (Philippians 3:5), a Pharisee (Acts 23:6), and that he had acquired Roman citizenship by some means. Paul later referred to this stating: "I was freeborn" (Acts 22:28). Like other Jewish boys, Paul was taught a trade in his young years, which, in his case, was the manufacture of tents (Acts 18:3). He apparently moved to Jerusalem while quite young (22:3) and there came under the tutorship of the renowned teacher Gamaliel. A brilliant and promising young man, Paul soon rose to a position of prominence in the religious hierarchy—perhaps even becoming a member of the Sanhedrin Court. He was a zealous defender of

Judaism; upon the rise of the Christian sect, Paul was given authority to persecute and destroy the Christians. This he did with great zeal, consenting even to sentences of prison and death for many of them (Acts 26:9-11).

Paul's life reached a turning point, however, when he had a personal encounter with Jesus Christ on the Damascus Road —an experience he referred to again and again throughout the remainder of his life. Thus, Paul the murderer became Paul the missionary. And the same zeal he had demonstrated in persecuting the Church was afterward channeled toward furthering its cause. Most of the information we have concerning the life and ministry of this remarkable man is contained in the Book of Acts and in the letters ascribed to him.

Although Paul was instrumental in establishing a number of churches on his three missionary journeys, it is unlikely that he established the Church at Rome. His letter to the Romans was written three or more years prior to his visit to Rome. Therefore, in all likelihood the Church there was established either by persons who were converted on the Day of Pentecost (Acts 2:10) and carried the gospel back to the imperial city or by converts of Paul or of other apostles. The membership of the Roman Church was predominantly Gentile (Romans 1:13; 11:13; 15:5, 6), and Paul was very anxious to minister in this church which had already become widely known (1:8).

The Epistle to the Romans has been widely acclaimed as one of the greatest books in the Bible. Martin Luther referred to it as "the perfect gospel" and urged his followers to memorize it. Coleridge said it was "the most profound work in existence." Undoubtedly, it is one of Paul's masterpieces and takes rank among the greatest books of the New Testament.

Paul sounded the keynote of Romans in 1:16, 17—"For I am not ashamed of the gospel of Christ: for it is the power of God unto salvation to every one that believeth; to the Jew first, and also to the Greek. For therein is the righteousness of God revealed from faith to faith, as it is written, the just shall live by faith."

The great themes of the Book of Romans include the following: The Judgment of God (1:18), The Universality of Sin (3:9-20), Justification (3:24), Propitiation (3:25), Faith (chapter 4), Original Sin (5:12), Spiritual Gifts (12:3-8), and Respect for Government (13:1-7).

The Epistle to the Romans was written at Corinth during Paul's three-month stay in Greece (Acts 20:2, 3). This was about the year 58 A.D. after Paul had been a Christian for about twenty years. It is believed that Phoebe, who belonged to the church at Cenchrea near Corinth (16:1), journeyed to Rome and delivered the letter personally to the saints there.

Key verses for memorization in the Book of Romans include 1:16, 17; 3:23, 24; 5:1; 5:8; 6:23; 8:1; 8:37; 10:9, 10; 10:13; 12:1, 2; 15:13.

1 CORINTHIANS

Author	Date of Writing	Theme	Key Personalities	Main Events
Paul	A.D. 57	Proper Christian Conduct	Paul, Sosthenes, Stephanus, Fortunatus, Achaicus, Timotheus, (Timothy)	Paul's Discipline for the Corinthian Church

The city of Corinth was located on a narrow isthmus between the Aegean and Adriatic Seas, about forty miles from Athens. In Paul's day it was the commercial metropolis of Greece and was one of the largest, richest, and most important cities of the Roman Empire. Through its harbors flowed the commerce of the world. It boasted a population of 400 thousand and was surpassed only by Rome, Alexandria, and Antioch. Corinth also contained an outdoor theater which accommodated twenty thousand people where athletic games, similar to the Olympics, were held. The city was notorious for its immorality and vice. Its gods were the gods of lust and pleasure. The great Temple of Aphrodite (the Greek goddess of love), with its one thousand prostitutes, symbolized the glaring debauchery of the masses. So licentious were the people that "to Corinthianize" came to mean "to practice fornication."

The message of Jesus Christ was first preached in Corinth by Paul on his second missionary journey (A.D. 50-52). During his eighteen-month residency in Corinth, Paul stayed with Aquila and Priscilla and formed a business partnership with them manufacturing and selling tents. Paul at first preached in the synagogue; however, opposition forced him to move next door to the house of Justus. Continued opposition by the Jewish community resulted in his being brought before Gallio, the Roman deputy, where he was charged with teaching contrary to Jewish law. Gallio subsequently dismissed the charge, regarding it as a religious dispute rather than a matter for the Roman courts. In spite of the intense opposition faced by Paul in Corinth, a strong church was established there. His ministerial activity was encouraged by a vision from the Lord in which he was told, "I am with thee, and no man shall set on thee to hurt thee: for I have much people in this city" (Acts 18:10).

Paul's first Epistle to the Corinthians was written from the city of Ephesus while on his third missionary journey. This was several years after the founding of the church at Corinth, around A.D. 57. An earlier letter, which has become lost to history, was also written by Paul to the Corinthians. He referred to this earlier letter in chapter 5, verse 9.

First Corinthians was written in response to several reports received from Corinth regarding problems that had surfaced in the Corinthian Church, namely factionalism (chapters 1-4), immorality (chapters 5; 6:9-20), legal disputes among Christians being taken to pagan courts (6:1-11), questions regarding marriage and separation (chapter 7), meats offered to idols (chapters 8-11:1), abuses of the Lord's Supper (11:17-34), spiritual gifts (chapters 12-14), and misunderstandings regarding the resurrection of the dead (chapter 15). Thus, Paul's purpose in writing to the Corinthians was to correct the moral and spiritual dilemma into which the Corinthian Church had lapsed. He dealt with each of the issues successively and decisively and concluded his book by announcing his intentions for a future visit to Corinth (16:5-7).

One of the distinctive features of 1 Corinthians is Paul's emphasis upon the Lordship of Christ. He used the title "Lord" in reference to Jesus on at least eight different occasions (1:31; 2:8, 16; 3:20; 4:4; 5:4, 5; 6:13, and others). Verses suitable for memorization include 1:18; 1:27; 2:4, 5; 6:20; 10:13; 15:57, 58. One of the best known and most loved passages in the entire Bible is Paul's immortal classic on the theme of love found in chapter 13. In this chapter, Paul listed no less than fifteen identifying characteristics of genuine love. It goes without saying that this passage is unsurpassed in beauty, inspiration, and literary excellence.

2 CORINTHIANS

Author	Date of Writing	Theme	Key Personalities	Main Events
Paul	A.D. 57	My grace is sufficient.	Paul, Timothy, Titus	Paul's Discipline of the Corinthian Church

Altogether, Paul penned four letters to the church at Corinth. They are as follows:

1. The "previous" letter, referred to in 1 Corinthians 5:9, which has been lost to history
2. 1 Corinthians, written in A.D. 57
3. The "sorrowful" letter, referred to in 2 Corinthians 2:4 and 7:8, which has also been lost
4. 2 Corinthians, written six to eight months after 1 Corinthians (A.D. 57)

After writing 1 Corinthians, Paul apparently made a quick visit to Corinth in an attempt to personally resolve the problems to which he addressed himself in his first letter (2 Corinthians 2:1; 12:14; 13:1, 2). Following this visit, he wrote the church a stern but sorrowful letter in a continuing effort to resolve the issues. This letter was delivered by Titus, and Paul had hoped to wait at Ephesus for Titus' report concerning the response of the people. However, difficulties arose at Ephesus which prompted him to leave the city ahead of schedule (Acts 20:1). Paul journeyed on to Macedonia where he met Titus and received his report, which was, for the most part, favorable (2:12, 13).

Although the Corinthian Church at this point was showing signs of recovery, there was still a rebellious minority which continued to challenge the apostleship and authority of Paul. Certain members of this power group posed as "apostles" and "ministers of Christ," being led by a ring leader who was especially obnoxious to Paul (10:7-11; 2:5-11; 11:13-

15, 23). In their efforts to discredit him, the dissidents not only questioned the validity of Paul's apostleship, but accused him of cowardice in sending letters rather than making a personal appearance. Fearing they were losing ground in their smear campaign, these wicked leaders then launched a personal attack against Paul, even ridiculing his appearance and mannerisms. Their despicable, unscrupulous character is reflected in their criticism that "his bodily presence is weak, and his speech contemptible" (10:10).

All of these factors combined prompted Paul to write 2 Corinthians. It is believed to have been written from Philippi, a city of Macedonia, in the autumn of A.D. 57. This letter contains many autobiographical glimpses into the life of the Apostle Paul (4:8-18; 11:22-33) and is perhaps the most personal of all his epistles. It reveals many facts about Paul's life not recorded elsewhere, such as his escape from Damascus in a basket (11:32, 33), his experience of being caught up to the third heaven (12:1-4), his thorn in the flesh (12:7), and his intense suffering (11:23-27). In 2 Corinthians Paul spoke of glorying or boasting thirty-one times, not because he was a braggart, but because he felt compelled to defend his ministry and the purity of his motives.

Both tender entreaty and severe rebuke characterize 2 Corinthians. Paul was encouraged by the improved conditions in Corinth, but was obviously tiring of the continued rebellion and harassment. On occasion, the tone of 2 Corinthians is one of extreme disappointment. He told the Corinthians, "I will very gladly spend and be spent for you; though the more abundantly I love you, the less I be loved" (12:15). In his concluding remarks, Paul urged the Corinthians to "be perfect, be of good comfort, be of one mind, live in peace; and the God of love and peace shall be with you" (13:11).

Key verses in 2 Corinthians include 2:14; 5:10, 17, 21; 8:9; 9:15; 12:9; and 13:14. The longest discussion on the theme of giving in the New Testament is contained in chapters eight and nine.

GALATIANS

Author	Date of Writing	Theme	Key Personalities	Main Events
Paul	A.D. 50	Christian Liberty	Paul	Paul's Defense of His Apostleship Paul's Discussion on Law Vs. Grace, Paul's Discourse on Life in the Spirit

Galatians has been called the Magna Charta of the Christian faith. The basic theme of this epistle is "Christian Liberty"— the word *liberty* is used on at least four different occasions (2:4; 5:1; and twice in 5:13). The keynote of Paul's letter to the Galatians is found in chapter five, verse 1— "Stand fast therefore in the liberty wherewith Christ hath made us free, and be not entangled again with the yoke of bondage."

The yoke of bondage to which Paul referred was the rite of circumcision, a significant religious practice among the Jews. From the time of Abraham, this practice had been regarded as a token of the covenant relationship between God and Israel and was required of all Jewish males (Leviticus 12:3). Slaves and proselytes to the Jewish faith were also required to subscribe to the practice (Genesis 17:12, 13; Exodus 12:48). The basic issue with which Paul dealt in his Epistle to the Galatians was whether Gentile Christians were required to conform to the practices of Jewish law, including the rite of circumcision. Certain Judaizers (Jewish Christians) insisted that the Gentiles were not saved unless they subscribed to the Mosaic Law. These false teachers made it their business to visit and unsettle the Gentile churches and were determined to place the Jewish trademark on the Christian faith.

The Apostle Paul stood adamantly against this position, insisting that "a man is not justified by the works of the law, but by the faith of Jesus Christ" (2:16).

The churches Paul addressed in this epistle were in all

probability those he had established on his first missionary journey—Antioch, Iconium, Lystra, and Derbe. They were located in the southern part of the Roman province of Galatia (Acts 13, 14). When Paul returned to Antioch (A.D. 49), he received a report that these churches were being disrupted by Judaizers. Shortly before the Jerusalem Council (A.D. 50), the apostle wrote his Epistle to the Galatians in an attempt to reinforce the great doctrine that salvation issues by grace through faith and is not dependent upon the works of the Law.

The Galatian Epistle may be subdivided as follows:

1. Paul's Defense of His Apostleship (chapters 1 and 2)
2. Paul's Discussion on Law Vs. Grace (3:1-5:12)
3. Paul's Discourse on Life in the Spirit (5:13-6:10)

In the last section of Paul's letter to the Galatians, the apostle presents a graphic contrast between the works of the flesh and the fruit of the Spirit. Listing seventeen evil works, he described the walk of the flesh as a self-centered, pleasure-seeking lifestyle that totally disregards the will of God. On the other hand, the walk of the Spirit is presented as one of contentment and completeness. It is also victorious and abundant; by continued submission to the leadership of the Spirit, the fruit of the Spirit will be produced in the Christian's life. The ninefold cluster of fruit as described by Paul includes love, joy, peace, longsuffering (patience), gentleness (kindness), goodness, faith, meekness (humility), temperance (self control).

The first three fruits (love, joy, peace) are manifestations of the believer's relationship to Christ. The second three (longsuffering, gentleness, goodness) are to be expressed in relationship to others. The third group (faith, meekness, temperance) are qualities necessary for living a victorious Christian life. What beautiful Christian graces!

Key verses in Paul's Epistle to the Galatians are 2:16, 20; 3:11; 4:4-7; 5:1, 22-25; 6:14.

EPHESIANS

Author	Date of Writing	Theme	Key Personalities	Main Events
Paul	A.D. 61	Unity of the Church	Paul, Tychicus	Paul's Emphasis Upon the Unity of Believers

Ephesians, Philippians, Colossians, and Philemon are referred to as "prison epistles," since Paul wrote them during his Roman imprisonment (Ephesians 3:1; Philippians 1:7; Colossians 4:10; Philemon 9). It is uncertain whether Paul was imprisoned once or twice in Rome, but many scholars agree that he suffered two imprisonments. The last chapter of Acts apparently refers to Paul's first imprisonment during which time he was under house arrest for a period of two years (Acts 28:30). In all probability, he wrote the four prison epistles during this time. After his release Paul made several trips, perhaps to Spain and other areas, and wrote 1 Timothy and Titus. He then was rearrested, finally suffering martyrdom under the wicked emperor Nero (A.D. 67).

The city of Ephesus in Paul's day was an important political, commercial, and religious center. It was situated at the junction of natural trade routes and was on the main route from Rome to the East. It boasted of Roman baths, a library and stadium, and one of the largest theaters of its day. The auditorium was semicircular and accommodated an audience of 24,500 persons. The Ephesians were an extremely idolatrous people, dedicated to the worship of the mother goddess, Diana. The famous Temple to Diana was an imposing structure—four times larger than the Parthenon at Athens—and ranked as one of the seven wonders of the world.

Many Jews with Roman citizenship resided at Ephesus and maintained a synagogue (Acts 18:19; 19:17). Paul first visited Ephesus on his return from his second missionary journey.

At that time he preached in the synagogue, leaving Aquila and Priscilla in Ephesus to continue the work (Acts 18:18-21). On his third missionary journey (A.D. 53-58), Paul labored three years in Ephesus, firmly establishing the Church there (Acts 19:1; 20:17-38). The tremendous impact of Paul's ministry upon the city of Ephesus is evidenced by the public burning of the books of magic by many who had been converted to Christ (Acts 19:19). His ministry, however, was not without opposition. Demetrius, the silversmith, whose profits from making silver shrines for the worship of Diana were greatly curtailed by the preaching of the apostle, instigated a riot which ultimately necessitated Paul's departure from the city. Timothy was left in charge of the young church and is often regarded as the first bishop of the church at Ephesus (1 Timothy 1:3). Paul had plans to visit the church at Ephesus again on his return trip from Europe (third missionary journey). But when his schedule would not permit it, he summoned the elders to meet him at Miletus, where a very touching reunion took place (Acts 20:17-38). Paul then journeyed on to Jerusalem where he was subsequently arrested, tried, and made his appeal to Caesar. With his appeal granted, he was then sent to Rome and imprisoned to await trial there. His Epistle to the Ephesians was written from Rome, approximately 61 A.D., and delivered by Tychicus to the Ephesian Church.

The basic theme of Paul's letter to the Ephesians is the unity of the church. Paul's strong belief in the universal appeal of the gospel motivated him to carry the message of Christ to both Jew and Gentile. As a result, he had witnessed the rise of a new spiritual community composed of different races and languages. With the seeds of division already sown by the Judaizers and by other church factions, Paul perhaps feared a serious breach in the church. He therefore appealed to believers everywhere to recognize their common bond in Christ. It is quite possible that the letter to the Ephesians was a circular letter, a copy of which was delivered to all the churches in Paul's circuit.

In underscoring the theme of church unity, Paul used several recurring words and phrases. The word *together* appears five times throughout the book (1:1; 2:5; 2:6; 2:22); the word *one* appears eight times (2:15; 2:16; 2:18; 4:4-6); and the phrase "in Christ" is used on ten different occasions (1:1, 3, 6, 12, 15, 20; 2:10, 13; 3:11; 4:21). Other important expressions include the phrase "in heavenly places," used four times (1:3, 20; 2:6; 3:10), and "riches," which appears five times (1:7; 2:7; 1:18; 3:16; 3:8).

Paul's letter to the Ephesians is indeed a book of spiritual riches. Every chapter contains glittering gems of profound truth. Of special significance are Paul's two great prayers for the Ephesians (1:15-23; 3:13-21), his emphasis on Christ's headship over the body (1:22, 23; 4:15, 16), his graphic portrayal of the Church as the temple of God (2:21, 22) and the bride of Christ (5:22-33), and his description of the Christian's armor (6:10-18).

Ephesians may be subdivided as follows:

1. Paul's Appeal for Church Unity (chapters 1-3)

2. Paul's Challenge to Consistent Christian Living (chapters 4-6)

PHILIPPIANS

Author	Date of Writing	Theme	Key Personalities	Main Events
Paul	A.D. 62	Joy	Paul, Timothy, Epaphroditus	Paul's Thank You Note, Humiliation and Exaltation of Christ, Paul's Personal Goals

The church at Philippi was founded by Paul on his second missionary journey and was the first church to be established by him in Europe (Acts 16). Philippi was an important city of Macedonia, named for its founder, King Phillip, who was the father of Alexander the Great. Paul's efforts in Philippi were prompted by a vision received while at Troas in which a man from Macedonia besought him to "come over into Macedonia and help us." His first converts in Philippi included Lydia (a businesswoman from the city of Thyatira) and her household, a young girl out of whom Paul cast an evil spirit, and the Philippian jailer and his household (Acts 16).

Paul was especially close to the members of the Philippian Church, as evidenced by the warmness and cordiality of this epistle. This church was perhaps Paul's best loved church, for it entered more sympathetically into his sufferings and needs than did any of the other churches he had established. On at least two occasions, the Philippians responded to Paul's needs with financial assistance (4:16) and, hearing of his confinement in Rome, sent Epaphroditus with yet another gift. Philippians, therefore, is a thank you note for the gift brought by Epaphroditus and a very personal letter of encouragement to the church at Philippi. Upon Epaphroditus' arrival in Rome, he became extremely ill and was near death (2:27). However, he was spared and upon his recovery, Paul sensed his desire to return home. Epaphroditus thus became the bearer of Paul's letter to the Philippians. It was written near the end of Paul's first imprisonment in Rome (approximately 62 A.D.).

The theme of Paul's letter to the Philippians is joy. The word *joy* or *rejoice* occurs in this epistle some sixteen times. Although a prisoner, the great apostle was still able to strike the keynotes of victory and joy. He reminded the Philippians of his joy in prayer (1:4), in the gospel (1:18), in Christian fellowship (2:1, 2), in sacrifice and service (2:17, 18), in the Lord (3:1), and in the thoughtfulness and concern of the church for him (4:10). One of the most important doctrinal passages in the New Testament is Philippians 2:5-8, in which Paul wrote of the humiliation and exaltation of Christ. Of special significance, also, is Paul's list of personal goals:

1. "That I may win Christ" (3:8)
2. "That I may know him" (3:10)
3. That I may "be found in him" (3:9)
4. That I may know "the power of his resurrection" (3:10)
5. That I may know "the fellowship of his sufferings" (3:10)
6. "That I may apprehend that for which also I am apprehended" (3:12)
7. That I may gain "the prize of the high calling of God in Christ Jesus" (3:14)

Favorite verses in this epistle include 1:21; 3:10; and 4:8. The secret of Paul's spiritual success is found in Philippians 4:13—"I can do all things through Christ which strengtheneth me."

COLOSSIANS

Author	Date of Writing	Theme	Key Personalities	Main Events
Paul	A.D. 62	The Pre-eminent Christ	Paul, Epaphras, Onesimus	Paul's Emphasis Upon the Supremacy and Lordship of Christ

The city of Colosse was located about one hundred miles east of Ephesus. In ancient times it was a thriving city, located on primary trade routes. However, after a change in the road system, the neighboring cities of Laodicea and Hierapolis (Colossians 2:1; 4:13) surpassed it in commercial importance. Since most of the Christians at Colosse had never met Paul (2:1), it is generally believed that Epaphras, Paul's coworker, was responsible for the founding of the church there (1:7). It is quite possible that Epaphras also evangelized the cities of Laodicea and Hierapolis (4:12, 13).

While some scholars believe the Epistle to the Colossians may have been written from Ephesus or Caesarea, it was most likely written from Rome during Paul's first imprisonment (A.D. 61-63). The letter was prompted by a visit from Epaphras in which Paul was informed of a strange mixture of false doctrine that had crept into the church at Colosse. Apparently Epaphras and his fellow workers were unable to cope with the situation and journeyed to Rome to consult Paul about it (1:7, 8). Epaphras, for unknown reasons, could not return to Colosse immediately (4:12; Philemon 23). Paul, therefore, sent the letter to the Colossians by the hand of Tychicus and Onesimus (4:7-9).

The heresy existing in the Colossian Church seems to have been a mixture of Jewish, Greek, and Oriental philosophy and religion. The Jewish element is seen in Paul's references to circumcision, meats and drinks, feast days, new moons, and sabbaths (2:11-16); the ascetic element is noted in the references to certain practices of the people—"Touch not; taste not; handle not" (2:21); the Greek element is seen in his warnings against "philosophy and vain deceit" (2:8). At the heart of the Colossian heresy was a growing belief in the worship of angels and that Christ himself was just one among many angelic beings (2:8, 20).

Paul's purpose, therefore, in writing to the Colossians, was to correct these mushrooming errors within the Church. This he did by establishing the preeminence of Christ over all things. This epistle is a beautiful defense of the supremacy and Lordship of Christ. His preeminence is portrayed as follows:

In His deity—"The image of the invisible God" (1:15)

In Creation—"By him were all things created" (1:16)

In His eternality—"He is before all things" (1:17)

In His power—"By him all things consist" (1:17)

In His Church—"He is the head of the body" (1:18)

In His redemptive work—"And, having made peace through the blood of his cross, by him to reconcile all things unto himself" (1:20)

In His resurrection and mediatorial work—"If ye then be risen with Christ, seek those things which are above, where Christ sitteth on the right hand of God" (3:1)

Also worthy of note in this letter is Paul's description of the believer's relationship to Christ—walking in Him (2:6), being rooted in Him (2:7), being built up in Him (2:7), being complete in Him (2:10), being dead with Him (2:20), being risen with Him (3:1), and being hidden with Him (3:3).

The Epistle to the Colossians may be subdivided as follows:

1. Introduction and Thanksgiving (1:1-8)
2. Doctrinal Section (1:9-3:4)
3. Practical Exhortations (3:5-4:6)
4. Concluding Salutations (4:7-18)

1 AND 2 THESSALONIANS

Author	Date of Writing	Theme	Key Personalities	Main Events
Paul	A.D. 51 or 52	The Second Coming of Christ	Paul, Silvanus (Silas), Timothy	Emphasis Upon the Second Coming of Christ

Paul's two letters to the Thessalonians are considered to be among the earliest of his writings. They were probably written in A.D. 51 or the early part of A.D. 52. The city of Thessalonica was located on the Aegean Sea within sight of Mount Olympus, commonly regarded as the home of the Greek gods. Thessalonica was a leading city of Macedonia in Paul's day and was a prosperous commercial center, much like Ephesus and Corinth.

The church at Thessalonica was established by Paul and his companions, Silas and Timothy, on the second missionary journey (Acts 17:1-14). After leaving Philippi where the first European church was founded amid severe persecution, Paul and his party journeyed to Thessalonica. The reception at Thessalonica was little better than it had been at Philippi. Paul's presence in the city soon created a great stir, and his enemies accused him of "[turning] the world upside down" (Acts 17:6). As was often the case, Paul's own people—the Jews—were his chief enemies. Following a riot instigated by the Jews and an assault on the house of Jason where Paul was lodging, he left the city after a stay of only three or four weeks (Acts 17:2). Although his ministry at Thessalonica was brief, it was fruitful nonetheless. Acts 17:4 indicates that a great multitude of devout Greeks believed (including a large number of prominent women), thus forming the nucleus of a strong church in that city. From Thessalonica Paul and his company first went to Berea and then to Athens. When they arrived in Athens, Paul sent Timothy back to Thessalonica (3:1, 2, 5) to encourage the believers and to secure a report on the condition of the church. Timothy rejoined Paul in Corinth (3:6) where the two Thessalonian letters were written.

The basic theme of both Thessalonian letters is the Second Coming of Christ, which Paul referred to some twenty times (1:10; 2:19; 3:13; 4:16-18; 5:23). Apparently some of the Thessalonians had misunderstood Paul's teaching concerning the Second Coming of Christ. Believing that Christ would return immediately, some had given up their work (1 Thessalonians 2:9; 4:11; 2 Thessalonians 3:8, 10-12) while others were conducting themselves in a disorderly fashion (1 Thessalonians 5:14; 2 Thessalonians 3:6, 7, 11). Still another group was worried and confused over the fate of those who die prior to the Second Coming of Christ (1 Thessalonians 4:13, 18). Paul, therefore, wrote his letters to quiet the fears of the people and to deal with the errors that had developed. Paul's first letter evidently did not sufficiently satisfy the issues, necessitating the second letter which followed a few months later. The first phase of Christ's advent, known as the "Rapture" (1 Thessalonians 4:13-18), is emphasized in 1 Thessalonians. The second phase, known in the Old Testament as "the day of the Lord," is stressed in 2 Thessalonians. Paul was careful to point out that the second aspect of Christ's coming follows the rise of the Antichrist (also called "man of sin," "the son of perdition,") and will be accompanied by judgment upon the ungodly (2 Thessalonians 1:7-10; 2:1-12).

In addition to his emphasis upon the Second Coming of Christ, Paul also used his letters to the Thessalonians as an occasion to defend himself against the allegation that his work was motivated by desire for profit (1 Thessalonians 2: 9, 10) and to encourage the Church to remain steadfast under the fires of persecution (1 Thessalonians 2:17-3:10).

137

These letters are very warm and personal and reflect the apostle's deep affection for the Thessalonian Christians. His special attachment to them is indicated in 1 Thessalonians 2:19, 20, where he described them as his hope, joy, crown of rejoicing, and glory.

1 AND 2 TIMOTHY

Author	Date of Writing	Theme	Key Personalities	Main Events
Paul	1 Timothy— A.D. 64 or 65, 2 Timothy— A.D. 67	1 Timothy— Fighting the Good Fight, 2 Timothy—A Good Soldier of Jesus Christ	Paul, Timothy	Paul's Guidelines for Pastors, Paul's Final Testimony to the World

Paul's two letters to Timothy and the one to Titus are frequently referred to as "pastoral epistles," primarily because they contain principles for pastoral care of churches and qualifications for ministers. These books are believed to have been written between Paul's first and second Roman imprisonments (between A.D. 63 and 67). In all probability, his first letter to Timothy was written in A.D. 64 or 65 and his second letter shortly before his death in A.D. 67.

Timothy was a native of Lystra (Acts 16:1), where Paul on one occasion was stoned and left for dead. Timothy was the son of a Jewish mother named Eunice and a Greek father whose name is unknown. His grandmother's name was Lois (2 Timothy 1:5). Timothy was converted under the ministry of the Apostle Paul, and a strong bond of affection developed between them. Paul frequently referred to young Timothy as his own son, calling him "my own son in the faith" (1 Timothy 1:2) and "my dearly beloved son" (2 Timothy 1:2). Timothy joined Paul on his second missionary journey and traveled extensively with him for a number of years. Later, Timothy was appointed to be in charge of the work in Ephesus and Asia Minor. This was quite a responsibility for such a young man, and apparently Timothy felt somewhat overwhelmed by the awesomeness of his charge. Being timid and retiring by nature and not in the best of health (1 Timothy 5:23), Timothy felt his need for the guiding hand of the older, wiser, and more experienced apostle.

The basic purpose, therefore, of Paul's first letter to Timothy was to provide specific directions for shepherding and supervising the church. The key verse states, "That thou mayest know how thou oughtest to behave thyself in the house of God" (3:15). Paul's guidelines are as follows:

1. Doctrinal Guidelines (1:3-20)
2. Worship Guidelines (2:1-15)
3. Leadership Guidelines (3:1-16)
4. Practical Guidelines (4:1-6:5)
5. Personal Guidelines (6:6-21)

Important subjects discussed in this epistle include the Law (1:7-11), prayer (2:1-8), appearance and activity of women (2:9-15), qualifications for bishops or elders and for deacons (3:1-13), the last days (4:1-3), care of widows (5:3-16), and the use of money (6:6-19).

Paul's second letter to Timothy is very personal in nature and is regarded as his last message to Timothy, to the Church, and to the world. After writing his first epistle to Timothy, Paul was arrested again in Greece or Asia Minor and brought back to Rome, this time as a criminal (2:9). During his first imprisonment in Rome, he had been accused of petty violations of Jewish laws; now he and thousands of other Christians had been arrested as enemies of the state of Rome. Under the wicked and bloodthirsty Nero, the Christians were hunted and herded like animals, falsely accused and given to the sword or the lions. On some occasions they were smeared with pitch and became flaming torches to light Nero's garden. Alone and cold in his dungeon (4:10-12), the veteran missionary sensed that his death was near. Therefore, he urged his son in the faith to "be strong in the grace that is in Christ Jesus" (2:1) and to be "a good soldier of Jesus Christ" (2:3). Paul's final testimony was not one of gloomy despair but rather one of victory and conquest. He stated: "For I am now ready to be offered, and the time of my departure is at hand. I have fought a good fight, I have finished my course, I have kept the faith" (2 Timothy 4:6, 7). Soon afterward (according to tradition), Paul was beheaded on the Ostian Way, west of Rome.

The second letter to Timothy not only includes personal instructions to Timothy and Paul's final testimony, but also a discussion of apostasy in the last days (3:1-9), the inspiration of the Scriptures (3:16), and the crown of righteousness (4:8), available to all who love the appearing of Christ.

Of special significance is Paul's use of the word *faithful* in his two letters to Timothy. This word appears on at least eight different occasions (1 Timothy 1:12, 15; 3:11; 4:9; 6:2; 2 Timothy 2:2, 11, 13) and is perhaps the one word that best characterizes the remarkable ministry of the great man Paul.

TITUS

Author	Date of Writing	Theme	Key Personalities	Main Events
Paul	A.D. 65	Good Works	Paul, Titus	Emphasis Upon Exemplary Christian Living, Instructions for the Management and Care of Churches

Like Paul's two letters to Timothy, Titus is regarded as a "pastoral epistle" due to its emphasis upon church care. At the time of this writing, Titus had been left on the island of Crete by Paul to superintend the work of the Church there (1:5). Details concerning the founding of the Church in Crete are sketchy. However, many scholars believe that it was established by the Cretes, who were present in Jerusalem on the Day of Pentecost (Acts 2:11). It is quite certain that Paul is not responsible for its founding, although his visit to Crete after his first Roman imprisonment undoubtedly contributed to its strength and growth (1:5). The island of Crete was located southeast of Greece on the border between the Aegean and Mediterranean Seas. It was approximately 150 miles long and seven to thirty miles wide. Dotted with mountains and fertile valleys, it was known as the "island of a hundred cities." Its highest mountain, Mount Ida, was famous as the legendary birthplace of the Greek god, Zeus.

Titus was a Gentile by birth (Galatians 2:3) and was converted through the ministry of the Apostle Paul (Titus 1:4). He subsequently became a close friend and companion of Paul and accompanied him to Jerusalem at the time of the Apostolic Council (Acts 15:2; Galatians 2:1-3). He was Paul's representative to the Corinthian Church and was apparently quite instrumental in helping solve the problems there (2 Corinthians 7:6, 7; 8:6, 16). He, along with another companion was responsible for the delivery of 2 Corinthians to the Church at Corinth and urged the Corinthians to respond to the collection for the poor at Jerusalem. Paul had implicit faith in the ability and leadership skills of Titus and referred to him as "my partner and fellowhelper" (2 Corinthians 8:23). Titus apparently was a strong personality and was quite adept in the areas of church management and organization.

Three things seem to have prompted the apostle to pen his letter to Titus:

1. The condition of the work in Crete
2. Titus' need of instruction and encouragement
3. The intention of Zenas and Apollos to visit the island of Crete

The basic theme of the letter is found in 3:8—"This is a faithful saying, and these things I will that thou affirm constantly, that they which have believed in God might be careful to maintain good works. These things are good and profitable unto men." Although Paul did not believe in "salvation by good works," it is most evident that he believed in "salvation unto good works." In this letter the phrase "good works" is mentioned at least six times (1:16; 2:7, 14; 3:1, 8, 14). In addition to Paul's emphasis upon good works, he used this letter to urge Titus to complete the organization of the work in Crete (1:5), to instruct him regarding the qualifications of elders (1:6-9), and to encourage Titus to take a strong stand against false teachers (1:10-16). Other subjects discussed in this letter include suggestions for dealing with various age groups within the Church (2:1-8), the importance of good citizenship (3:1, 2), and various doctrinal themes—salvation, justification, and eternal life (3:5-7). Verses suitable for memorization in Paul's letter to Titus are 2:11-13 and 3:5-7.

PHILEMON

Author	Date of Writing	Theme	Key Personalities	Main Events
Paul	A.D. 61	Forgiveness	Paul, Philemon, Onesimus	Paul's Intercession for Onesimus

Like Ephesians, Philippians, and Colossians, Philemon is commonly regarded as one of Paul's "prison epistles," written during his first confinement in Rome (A.D. 61-63). Philemon was converted under the ministry of the Apostle Paul and was a prominent member of the Church at Colosse (verse 19). Aside from the information supplied by Paul, very little is known regarding the background of Philemon. However, in this epistle Paul portrayed him as a man of outstanding character. He referred to Philemon as a "fellow-labourer" (verse 1) and spoke of his love, faith, and kindness toward the saints (verses 5-7). That he was a man of generous hospitality is indicated by Paul's request to lodge with him on a future visit (verse 22). Paul's reference to "the church in thy house" further indicates that Philemon had opened his home as a meeting place for Christian worship (verse 2).

The basic purpose for Paul's letter to Philemon was to intercede for a runaway slave named Onesimus, whom Paul had won to Christ during his confinement at Rome. Slavery was one of the terrible curses of the ancient world. Some Roman masters owned from ten to a thousand slaves who had no individual rights of life or liberty under Roman law. The practice of slavery was so widespread it has been estimated that there were as many as sixty million slaves throughout the Roman Empire. While Paul's letter to Philemon is not a comprehensive discussion of the problem of slavery, it did provide Christian principles for dealing with a massive social evil of those times. It also points out that slavery can never be the fruit of a truly Christian society. Onesimus was one of Philemon's slaves and being a "Phrygian," he was a slave of the lowest order. In the eyes of the law, he had no rights; perhaps Onesimus had also concluded that he had no responsibilities. Not only did he run away from his master, but he apparently robbed him prior to leaving (verse 18). Onesimus then went to Rome where he came in contact with the apostle, was converted, and became an attendant to Paul in his bonds.

Paul would have gladly kept Onesimus with him in Rome. However, he did not feel it would be right for him to do so without Philemon's consent. Even though Onesimus had repented, he had not made restitution for his wrongs. Upon Tychicus' return to Asia with Paul's Epistles to the Ephesians and the Colossians, Onesimus was sent with him, bearing this beautiful letter of intercession.

Paul's letter to Philemon is one of the most personal letters penned by his hand. Though brief (consisting of only twenty-five verses), it is nonetheless a masterpiece. It is a true gem of courtesy and tact and reveals much about the feelings, personality, and noble character of the author.

HEBREWS

Author	Date of Writing	Theme	Key Personalities	Main Events
Uncertain	A.D. 67-69	The Superiority of Christ	Moses, Joshua, Aaron, Melchisedec, Heroes/Heroines of Faith (Chapter 11)	Discussion of Christ's Superiority (Chapters 1-10), Practical Exhortations in Christian Living (Chapters 11-13)

For centuries the authorship of Hebrews has been the subject of great controversy. Some authorities have ascribed it to Paul, while others believe it to have been written by Apollos, Silas, Barnabas, Luke, Aquila and Priscilla, and various other persons. Since the author remains unidentified in the book itself, the most accurate conclusion which can be drawn is that of the third century theologian Origen who said, "Only God knows who wrote Hebrews."

The Book of Hebrews is believed to have been written prior to the fall of Jerusalem (A.D. 70). Although an exact date cannot be determined, a generally accepted date for its writing is A.D. 67-69. The key word in the Book of Hebrews is *better*, occurring some thirteen times. The writer spoke of better things (6:9; 12:24), a better hope (7:19), a better testament (7:22), a better covenant (8:6), better promises (8:6), better sacrifices (9:23), a better country (11:16), and a better resurrection (11:35). The words *perfection* and *heavenly* also appear frequently throughout the book.

As indicated by the title and subject matter, Hebrews was addressed primarily to a Jewish audience—perhaps the Jewish saints at Jerusalem and in the surrounding area. Apparently a large segment of Jewish Christians was continuing the practices and rituals of the Levitical system of worship. They had not clearly understood that Christ "had offered one sacrifice for sins for ever" (10:12) and had in fact instituted "a new and living way" (10:20). Therefore, a clear purpose of the Book of Hebrews is to identify the transition from the old system to the new and to portray Christ as the total fulfillment of those things prefigured in the Old Testament. There are twenty-nine direct quotations from the Old Testament and an additional fifty-three allusions to it.

The obvious theme of the Book of Hebrews is "The Superiority of Christ." The author skillfully and effectively contrasted the person and ministry of Jesus Christ with the requirements of the Old Testament sacrificial system and showed how He is superior in every way. As a leader, He is greater than the prophets (1:1-3), greater than angels (1:4-2:18), greater than Moses (3:1-19), and greater than Joshua (4:1-16). As a priest, He is superior to Aaron and is said to be "a priest for ever after the order of Melchisedec" (5:6). As to the work and ministry of Christ, He is portrayed as "the mediator of the new testament" (9:15) and the perfect sacrifice for sin (10:1-20). Thus, the first ten chapters of Hebrews focus upon the person, priesthood, and propitiation of Christ. The last three chapters are dedicated to practical exhortations which include, among other things, the hall of faith (chapter 11), the Christian race (12:1, 2), social and moral responsibility (13:1-7), and the author's great benediction (13:20, 21).

Also of particular interest in the Book of Hebrews are the "let us" phrases. Eleven in number, they are as follows: "fear" (4:1), "labour" (4:11), "come boldly unto the throne of grace" (4:16), "go on unto perfection" (6:1), "draw near" (10:22), "hold fast" (10:23), "consider one another" (10:24), "Lay aside every weight . . . and run with patience" (12:1), "have grace" (12:28), "go forth" (13:13), and "offer the sacrifice of praise" (13:15).

As a literary work, Hebrews is superb. Not only is it written in an interesting and inspiring manner, but it often rises to the heights of profound eloquence. Because of its majestic description of Christ, it has often been called the "Isaiah" of the New Testament. A journey through the pages of Hebrews is unquestionably a rich and rewarding experience!

REVIEW — UNIT 7

(Romans—Hebrews)

1. Write a brief paragraph about the life of Paul.
2. The theme of Romans is _____.
3. _____ _____ called Romans "the perfect gospel."
4. The membership of the Roman Church was predominantly _____.
5. Name three great doctrines taught in the Book of Romans.
6. The Epistle to the Romans was written at _____ and delivered to the Church at Rome by _____.
7. Paul first preached in Corinth on his _____ missionary journey.
8. While at Corinth Paul lived with _____ and _____.
9. List three problems existing in the Church at Corinth cited by Paul.
10. The title _____, used in reference to Jesus, appears _____ times in 1 Corinthians.
11. Altogether, Paul wrote _____ letters to the Church at Corinth.
12. Galatians has been called the _____ _____ of the Christian faith.
13. The theme of Galatians is _____ _____.
14. List the nine fruits of the Spirit.
15. List the four books referred to as "prison epistles."
16. The theme of Ephesians is _____.
17. _____ brought a gift from the Philippian Church to Paul when he was imprisoned in Rome.
18. The heresy to which Paul addressed himself in his letter to the Colossians was a mixture of _____, _____, and _____ philosophy and religion.

19. Paul's two letters to the _____ are considered to be among the earliest of his writings.

20. Name the three "pastoral epistles."

21. The basic theme of the Thessalonian letters is _____.

22. The name of Timothy's mother was _____; his grandmother's name was _____.

23. Titus was in charge of the churches on the Island of _____ when Paul wrote his letter to him.

24. In Paul's letter to Titus, the phrase _____ _____ appears at least six times.

25. The basic purpose for Paul's letter to Philemon was to intercede for a runaway slave named _____.

26. _____ said, "Only God knows who wrote Hebrews."

27. A key word appearing some thirteen times in the Book of Hebrews is _____.

28. In Hebrews, Christ is described as being "a priest for ever after the order of _____."

29. Hebrews is sometimes referred to as the _____ of the New Testament.

30. List three of Paul's personal goals given in his letter to the Philippians.

UNIT 8

JAMES

Author	Date of Writing	Theme	Key Personalities	Main Events
James— The Brother of Jesus	A.D. 45-48	Doers of the Word	James	Emphasis Upon the Practical Aspects of Christianity

The seven letters of James, Peter, John, and Jude comprise a group of New Testament writings known as the "general epistles." In the early church they were also called "catholic" or "universal" epistles because they (unlike the Pauline Epistles) were not addressed to individual churches or persons.

There is some uncertainty regarding the authorship of this book since no less than four men in the New Testament bear the name James—James, the son of Zebedee (Matthew 4:21), James, the son of Alphaeus, also called "the little" or "the less" (Matthew 10:3; Mark 15:40), James, the brother of Judas the apostle—not Iscariot (Luke 6:16), and the Lord's brother (Matthew 13:55; Galatians 1:19).

Inasmuch as James, the son of Zebedee, was killed by Herod Agrippa I (A.D. 44) and the other two men are rather inconspicuous personalities in the New Testament, it is generally believed that James, the brother of Jesus, is the author of this epistle.

James was in reality a half-brother of the Lord, having the same mother but not the same father (Matthew 13:55; Mark 6:3). He appears to have been an unbeliever for several years (John 7:5, 10), but Christ's personal appearance to him following the Resurrection became the turning point of his life (1 Corinthians 15:7). He was next seen in the Upper Room at Pentecost (Acts 1:14) and thereafter quickly arose to a place of prominence in the Church. James was recognized very early as the bishop of the Church at Jerusalem. The scope of his leadership is seen in Peter's reporting to him after his release from prison (Acts 12:17), Paul's respect for his advice (Acts 21:18), and his presiding over the Jerusalem Council (Acts 15:13, 19; Galatians 2:1, 9, 10). James was not only an outstanding church leader, but a devout Christian. So exemplary was his life and character that he became widely known as "James the just."

The keynote of the epistle is •1:22—"But be ye doers of the word, and not hearers only, deceiving your own selves." James was a very practical man, and he obviously viewed and interpreted the Christian faith in terms of its practical relationship to everyday life experiences. To put it in contemporary terms, James believed in "practicing what you preach." While some books of the Bible emphasize doctrine, this epistle emphasizes deeds. Faith and works are viewed by the author as inseparable twins; the manifestation of one without the other reflects imbalance and incompleteness in the Christian experience (2:14-26).

Due to the wide variety of practical subjects discussed in this epistle, it is sometimes called the "Proverbs" of the New Testament. The book covers such topics as temptation, patience, wisdom, prayer, poverty, riches, lust, sin, faith, good works, respect of persons, sins of the tongue, worldly mindedness, origin of wars, and self-sufficiency. Out of the 108 verses of the book, there are references or allusions to twenty-two books of the Old Testament and at least fifteen allusions to the teachings of Christ found in the Sermon on the Mount. Favorite verses include 1:5, 12, 17, 22; 2:17; 3:16-18; 4:8; 5:8, 13-16.

It is interesting that the Epistle of James begins and ends with a strong emphasis upon prayer (1:6; 5:14-18). History records that the author himself was a man given to prayer. It is said of James that he spent so much time on his knees they became hard and calloused like a camel's knees. James suffered martyrdom about A.D. 62 by the order of

Ananus, the high priest. According to Hegesippus, as quoted in the writings of Eusebius (A.D. 260-340), James was thrown headlong from the pinnacle of the Temple, then stoned and clubbed to death by the Pharisees and their followers. Like those of Jesus, his dying words were, "Father, forgive them for they know not what they do."

1 AND 2 PETER

Author	Date of Writing	Theme	Key Personalities	Main Events
The Apostle Peter	1 Peter— A.D. 63, 2 Peter —A.D. 66	1 Peter— Steadfastness in Suffering, 2 Peter —Warnings Against False Teachers	The Apostle Peter	Peter's Encouragement of the Suffering Saints, Peter's Condemnation of False Teachers

The Apostle Peter, author of these two epistles, is one of the best known personalities in the New Testament. He is variously identified as Simon, son of Jona (or Jonas, John 1:42; 21:16), Simon Peter (2 Peter 1:1), and Cephas, a name given to him by Jesus which meant "rock." Peter and his brother Andrew were fishermen on the Sea of Galilee and were in partnership with the sons of Zebedee (Matthew 4:18; Mark 1:16; Luke 5:3). He was a native of Bethsaida (John 1:44), but later moved with his family to Capernaum (Matthew 8:14; Luke 4:38).

Peter was, in all probability, a disciple of John the Baptist and was first introduced to Jesus by his brother Andrew. Jesus immediately recognized the potential of Peter and subsequently selected him to become one of the Twelve (Matthew 4:19; 10:2). His eager and courageous disposition marked Peter as a leader among the disciples from the very beginning. His name always heads the list of apostles (Matthew 10:2; Mark 3:16; Luke 6:14; Acts 1:13) and also appears first among the three "inner circle disciples" (Matthew 17: 1; Mark 5:37; 9:2; 13:3; 14:33; Luke 8:51; 9:28). Peter was the natural spokesman for the apostolic band and was the first to confess Jesus as the Christ of God.

Although Simon Peter was a man of remarkable quality, he

was not without his faults. The scriptural record not only points out his successes but also his failures. Peter's denial of Christ during the bitter hour of the Cross was, without doubt, one of the saddest events of the New Testament. After his genuine repentance, however, and following the reality of Christ's resurrection, Simon Peter became a new man. At Pentecost his sermon was instrumental in the conversion of three thousand people. He also became a powerful leader of the early church. It was by his voice that Ananias and Saphira were rebuked (Acts 5:1-11) and by his hand that the door for preaching the gospel to the Gentiles was first opened (Acts 10). His later ministry took him to Antioch (Galatians 2:11), possibly to Corinth (1 Corinthians 1:12), and probably to Rome where it is believed he suffered martyrdom by crucifixion (A.D. 67). According to tradition, Peter, at the hour of his death, felt unworthy to die in the same manner as did his Lord and requested that he be crucified with his head downward.

The First Epistle of Peter was written in approximately A.D. 63. It was addressed to the strangers (literally "sojourners of the dispersion"—1:1) scattered throughout the five provinces of Asia Minor—Pontus, Galatia, Cappadocia, Asia, and Bithynia. Many of the churches in this area were established by Paul, although Peter himself may have visited and preached in some of the provinces. The congregations were predominantly Gentile (1:14; 2:9, 10; 4:3, 4) and were undergoing a terrible siege of persecution at the time of Peter's writing. The word *suffering* (or its derivative) appears some sixteen times throughout the epistle, thus denoting the severity of the situation.

The purpose of Peter's first letter, therefore, was to encourage the "elect" (Christians) to remain steadfast under trial and to assure them of the sufficiency of God's grace. The grace of God is referred to at least eight times in the 105 verses of the epistle (1:2, 10, 13; 3:7; 4:10; 5:5, 10, 12). The marvelous grace of which Peter speaks may be outlined as follows: Grace for Salvation (1:2), Grace for

Suffering (1:13, 21), Grace for Service (4:10), and Grace for Steadfastness (5:10). Other key words of this epistle include *hope* used four times (1:3, 13, 21; 3:15) and *precious* occurring six times (1:7; 1:19; 2:4, 6, 7; 3:4). Verses suitable for memorization include 1:23; 2:7, 9; 3:18; 5:7.

While the emphasis of 1 Peter is upon suffering, the emphasis of 2 Peter is upon false teachers. When Peter penned his first letter, the major problems of the Church were from without; when he wrote the second a few years later, they were from within. Therefore, 1 Peter is a book of consolation; 2 Peter is one of warning.

The false teachers to whom Peter referred were probably the same as those condemned by John and Jude (see overviews of the Epistles of John and Jude). They taught a form of gnosticism which denied the deity of Christ (2:1), questioned the validity and authority of the Scriptures (1:16-21), and scoffed at the idea of Christ's Second Coming (3:1-4). They were morally corrupt, self-willed, and disrespectful of apostolic leadership (2:10). Peter severely condemned these wicked troublemakers and urged the Church to combat their false doctrines by possessing a genuine knowledge of the truth. The key verse of 2 Peter is 3:18—"But grow in grace, and in the knowledge of our Lord and Saviour Jesus Christ."

Both Epistles of Peter are believed to have been written from Rome, the first being delivered to the churches of Asia Minor by Silvanus (better known as Silas). The manner of distribution for the second is unknown.

THE EPISTLES OF JOHN

Author	Date of Writing	Theme	Key Personalities	Main Events
The Apostle John	A.D. 90-95	1 John—Victorious Faith, 2 John—Walking in the Commandments of Christ, 3 John—Christian Hospitality	The Apostle John, Gaius, Diotrephes, Demetrius	John's Emphasis Upon Things "We Know," Exposure of False Teachers / Teachings, The Walk of Truth, Christian Hospitality

Authorship for these epistles is generally ascribed to John the apostle. He also wrote the Gospel of John and the Book of Revelation. (See the overview of the Gospel of John for information on the author's background.)

Like Peter and Jude, John was aware of the growing influence of false teachers within the ranks of the Church. These false teachers, known as gnostics, were corrupting the gospel and undermining the faith of many. The purpose of John's Epistles, therefore, was to counter the false doctrine and to undergird the faith of the saints.

True to his character and nature, John's first epistle is both tender and tough. While referring to the believers by affectionate titles such as "little children" (2:1, 18, 28; 3:7, 18; 4:4; 5:21) and "beloved" (3:2, 21; 4:1, 7, 11), he nevertheless struck hard at the doctrines and practices that were corrupting and destroying the Church. The key word in this epistle is *know*, which (along with its derivatives) appears over thirty times. For this reason, 1 John has often been called "the epistle of certainties." John was deeply devoted to Christ, and his stance toward the Christian faith was positive and unshakeable. He apparently hoped to instill the same set of values in the hearts of those to whom he wrote. Some of the things John says "we know" are as follows: We know that Christ came to take away our sins (3:5); "We know we have passed from death unto life" (3:14), "[We] know that [we] have eternal life" (5:13); We know that our prayers are answered (5:15).

This epistle is also a book of contrasts—light and darkness (1:6, 7; 2:8-11), love of the world and love of God (2:15-17), children of God and children of the devil (3:4-10), the Spirit of God and the spirit of Antichrist (4:1-3), love and hate (4:7-12, 16-21). Also of particular interest in 1 John are his descriptions of the nature of God—light (1:5), love (4:8, 16), life (5:11, 12), and righteousness (2:29). The keynote of 1 John is found in 5:4—"For whatsoever is born of God overcometh the world: and this is the victory that overcometh the world, even our faith." Verses suitable for memorization in 1 John include 1:7, 9; 2:15-17; 3:22; 4:10, 19; 5:14, 15.

The Second Epistle of John is addressed to the "elect lady and her children." Some authorities believe the elect lady referred to is a particular church; others believe the letter was addressed to an individual Christian and her family. The circumstances and subject material of 2 John are similar to those of the first epistle and were probably written from the same place—Ephesus. The primary emphasis of 2 John is an exhortation to walk in the commandments of Christ.

The Third Epistle of John is addressed to Gaius, for whom John had great personal respect. His identity cannot be positively determined, since there are several persons by this name in the New Testament. However, it is believed that the Gaius of whom Paul spoke (Romans 16:23) is the same man to whom John wrote. The basic theme of 3 John is "Christian Hospitality." The short letter of fourteen verses commended Gaius for his generous hospitality toward the brethren of the ministry and at the same time issued a sharp rebuke to a self-assertive church leader named Diotrephes, who refused to accommodate the visiting brethren. The letter may have been delivered to Gaius by Demetrius (verse 12), who himself could have been a traveling teacher.

JUDE

Author	Date of Writing	Theme	Key Personalities	Main Events
Jude	A.D. 70-80	Contend for the faith.	Jude	Denunciation of False Teachers, Exhortations to Believers

The author of this epistle identifies himself in the opening
verse as "the servant of Jesus Christ, and brother of James."
It is generally believed that the James to whom he referred
was the leader of the Jerusalem Church, author of the Epistle
of James, and half-brother of Jesus. This being true, Jude
(English form of Judas) would also be a half-brother of the
Lord (Matthew 13:55; Mark 6:3). There are at least six
other persons in the New Testament who are identified by
the same name (Luke 3:30; Acts 5:37; Mark 3:19; Acts 9:
11; Acts 15:22; Luke 6:16—also compare Acts 1:13; John
14:22). However, a careful sifting of biblical and historical
facts seems to exclude each of these for serious consideration
as the author of this epistle.

Unfortunately, little is known about the life of Jude. He
apparently was one of the younger brothers of Jesus and,
along with the rest of his brothers, disbelieved in the deity
of Christ until after the Resurrection (John 7:3-8). On the
Day of Pentecost several members of Jude's family were
present in the Upper Room, including his mother Mary and
his brethren (Acts 1:14). He was a less conspicuous personality than was James and, in all probability, confined his
ministry to the nation of Israel.

The basic purpose for Jude's Epistle was to warn against
false teachers and false doctrines that were threatening the
life of the Church. Jude had originally planned to write a
treatise on the Doctrine of Salvation (verse 3), but the havoc
being wrought by the false teachers became the subject of
greater urgency. Jude's Epistle, though brief (twenty-five

verses in length), is a powerful defense for the true faith of the gospel. He urged the Church to "earnestly contend for the faith which was once delivered unto the saints" (verse 3). With the boldness of a lion he attacked the false teachers and exposed their poisonous doctrines.

He described them as deceitful (verse 3), abusers of the grace of God (verse 4), deniers of Jesus Christ (verse 4), morally corrupt (verses 7, 8), rebellious (verse 8), ignorant (verse 10), potential murderers (verse 11), greedy (verse 11), murmurers, complainers, pleasure seekers, full of flattery, selfish (verse 16), ungodly, and sensual (verses 18, 19). He further described them as "spots in your feasts of charity . . . clouds . . . without water . . . trees . . . without fruit . . . raging waves of the sea . . . wandering stars" (verses 12, 13). The above description of the character of evildoers is without doubt the most graphic found anywhere in the Scriptures.

After effectively exposing the false teachers, Jude then exhorted believers to do four things (verses 20, 21):

1. Build up themselves on their most holy faith

2. Pray in the Holy Ghost

3. Keep themselves in the love of God

4. Look for the mercy of the Lord Jesus Christ unto eternal life

The benediction of Jude is one of the grandest in the Bible:

"Now unto him that is able to keep you from falling, and to present you faultless before the presence of his glory with exceeding joy, To the only wise God our Saviour, be glory and majesty, dominion and power, both now and ever. Amen" (verses 24, 25).

REVIEW — UNIT 8

(James—Jude)

1. Name the seven books known as "general epistles."
2. In the early church, these epistles were also known as _____ or _____ because they were not addressed to individual churches or persons.
3. While some books of the Bible emphasize doctrine, James emphasizes _____.
4. The Book of James begins and ends with a strong emphasis upon _____.
5. While the emphasis of 1 Peter is upon _____, the emphasis of 2 Peter is upon _____ _____.
6. The false doctrine which Peter, John, and Jude condemned was _____ which, among other things, denied the deity of Christ.
7. The Epistle of 1 Peter was delivered by _____ to the churches of Asia Minor.
8. The key word in 1 John is _____, which appears over thirty times.
9. First John has been called "the epistle of _____."
10. The Second Epistle of John is addressed to the _____ _____ and her children.
11. The Third Epistle of John is addressed to _____.
12. _____ was a self-assertive church leader who refused to demonstrate Christian hospitality to the brethren of the ministry.
13. _____ and _____ were half-brothers of Jesus.
14. _____ had originally planned to write a treatise on the doctrine of _____, but the havoc being wrought by false teachers became the subject of greater urgency.
15. "Contend for the _____" was the theme of _____'s Epistle.

UNIT 9

REVELATION

Author	Date of Writing	Theme	Key Personalities	Main Events
The Apostle John	A.D. 95-96	The Triumphant Christ	Jesus Christ, The Apostle John	Description of the Risen Lord, Messages to the Seven Churches, Events to Follow the Second Coming of Christ

Throughout the centuries, the Book of Revelation has been the subject of endless discussion and controversy. Thousands of books have been written to explain its meaning. Yet, it was never intended to be a book of mystery—but a "revealing" or "unveiling" of "things which must shortly come to pass" (1:1). Contrary to popular opinion, the Revelation is not that of the author but of Jesus Christ himself. Thus, when reading and studying this book, one should concentrate upon the activity of the risen Lord.

Authorship for the Revelation is usually ascribed to the Apostle John. Four times throughout the book, he identified himself as John (1:1, 4, 9; 22:8). The things which John recorded were given to him by Jesus Christ while he was exiled on Patmos (1:9)—a rocky, barren island about sixty miles southwest of Ephesus. John is said to have been banished there during the persecution of Domitian, A.D. 95, and to have been released and permitted to return to Ephesus under the following emperor Nerva, A.D. 96.

With the outline suggested in 1:19, the Book of Revelation falls naturally into three divisions:

1. "The things which thou hast seen" (1:9-20)
2. "The things which are" (2:1-3:22)
3. "The things which shall be hereafter" (4:1-22:5)

Under the first section, John discussed the circumstances of his vision and presented a glorious view of the risen Christ. The second section contains messages to the seven churches of Asia Minor. The third section primarily consists of events which will transpire following the Second Coming of Christ. They include the seven-year tribulation, defeat of the Antichrist, establishment of the millennial reign of Christ, the Great White Throne Judgment, and the consummation of all things.

Of particular interest in the Book of Revelation are the "seven seven's," which are as follows: seven churches, seven seals, seven trumpets, seven personages, seven vials, seven dooms, and seven new things.

Also of particular interest are the Seven Beatitudes of Revelation, which are as follows:

1. "Blessed is he that readeth . . . this prophecy" (1: 3).
2. "Blessed are the dead who die in the Lord" (14:13).
3. "Blessed is he that watcheth [for the Lord's Coming]" (16:15).
4. "Blessed are they which are called unto the marriage supper of the Lamb" (19:9).
5. "Blessed . . . is he that hath part in the first resurrection" (20:6).
6. "Blessed is he that keepeth the sayings of the prophecy of this book" (22:7).
7. "Blessed are they that do his commandments" (22:14).

It has been said that there are at least three hundred symbols in this book, each of which has a significant meaning. For a clearer understanding of the Book of Revelation, it should be studied in conjunction with Matthew 24 and the prophecies of Ezekiel, Daniel, and Zechariah. A key word in the Book of Revelation is *lamb*, a sacrificial title referring to Christ. It occurs no less than twenty-six times throughout the book.

As Genesis is the book of beginnings, so Revelation is the book of consummation. It is the grand finale of God's plan for man, the Church, and the ages. Genesis records the creation of the heaven and the earth, but Revelation records the creation of a new heaven and a new earth. In Genesis the sun and moon appear, but in Revelation there will no longer be need for them, for Christ himself will be the light of the new heaven. In Genesis there is a beautiful garden, but in Revelation there is a more perfect place—the holy city of God. In Genesis there is the uniting of the first man, Adam, and the first woman, Eve, in marriage. But in Revelation there is the marriage of the second Adam—Jesus Christ—to His bride—the Church. In Genesis we have the entrance of sin, but in Revelation all sin is removed. In Genesis we see Satan rearing his ugly head for the first time, but in Revelation man's greatest adversary is eternally destroyed. In Genesis we have the beginning of sorrow, pain, death, and tears. But in Revelation the former things are passed away and God himself shall heal every sorrow and dry every tear.

Little wonder then that the Book of Revelation has been described as the "greatest drama of all time." It is a thrilling adventure to peruse the pages of this wonderful book and capture the panoramic view of the final scenes of world history. Jesus Christ is the Hero; the devil is the villain. And it is comforting to know the outcome of the struggle. Jesus Christ will unquestionably emerge the Victor. What a glorious day when "the kingdoms of this world are become the kingdoms of our Lord, and of his Christ; and he shall reign for ever and ever" (11:15)!

REVIEW — UNIT 9

(Revelation)

1. Authorship for the Book of Revelation is ascribed to
_____.

2. Contrary to popular opinion, the Revelation referred to is not that of the author but of _____ _____.

3. When John received the Revelation, he was exiled on the Island of _____.

4. The title "Revelation" means _____.

5. List the "seven seven's" that appear in the Book of Revelation.

6. The Book of Revelation falls naturally into _____ divisions.

7. Discuss briefly the basic contents of the divisions of the book.

8. The seven statements beginning with the word *blessed* are known as the _____ of Revelation.

9. For a clearer understanding of Revelation, it should be studied in conjunction with the twenty-fourth chapter of _____ and the prophecies of _____, _____, and _____.

10. Write a paragraph contrasting the Book of Genesis with the Book of Revelation.

Bibliography

Bell, Alvin E., *The Gist of the Bible*. Grand Rapids: Zondervan, 1961.

Burdick, Donald W., *The Epistles of John*. Chicago: Moody Press, 1970.

Coder, S. Maxwell, *Jude—The Acts of the Apostates*. Chicago: Moody Press, 1958.

Conn, Charles W., *Christ and the Gospels*. Cleveland, Tennessee: Pathway Press, 1964.

Conn, Charles W., *Highlights of Hebrew History*. Cleveland, Tennessee: Pathway Press, 1975.

Cramer, George H., *First and Second Peter*. Chicago: Moody Press, 1967.

Davis, John D., *The Westminster Dictionary of the Bible*. Philadelphia: Westminster Press, 1944.

Evans, William, *Outline Study of the Bible*. Chicago: Moody Press, 1941.

Freeman, Hobart E., *An Introduction to the Old Testament Prophets*. Chicago: Moody Press, 1977.

Halley, Henry H., *Pocket Bible Handbook*. Chicago: 1946.

Luck, G. Coleman, *James—Faith In Action*. Chicago: Moody Press, 1954.

Mears, Henrietta C., *What the Bible Is All About*. Glendale: Gospel Light Publications, 1953.

Purkiser, W. T., *Know Your Old Testament*. Kansas City: Beacon Hill Press, 1947.

Ryrie, Charles Caldwell, *The Acts of the Apostles*. Chicago: Moody Press, 1961.

Ryrie, Charles Caldwell, *The Ryrie Study Bible*. Chicago: Moody Press, 1976.

Smith, William, *Dictionary of the Bible*. Philadelphia: Universal Book and Bible House, 1948.

Thiessen, Henry Clarence, *Introduction to the New Testament*. Grand Rapids: Wm. B. Eerdmans Publishing Company, 1950.

Thompson, Frank Charles, *The New Chain Reference Bible*. Indianapolis: B. B. Kirkbride Bible Co., Inc., 1957.